T0303010

SALTWATER FLY FISHING
Seven Strategies for Success

CAPT. MIKE STARKE

DRAWINGS BY RICK BENDER

BURFORD BOOKS

To my beautiful wife Patty
for always being there,

understanding my other passion in life
and for helping me realize my dreams.

Printed in the United States of America.

10 9 8 7 6 5 4 3 2 1

Front cover photo by Greg and Carol Mentzer.
All photos and computer illustrations by the author,
unless otherwise noted.
Artwork and line illustrations by Rick Bender.

Library of Congress Cataloging-in-Publication Data
Starke, Michael G.
    Saltwater fly fishing : seven strategies for success / Michael G. Starke.
        p. cm.
    ISBN 1-58080-102-1 (hardcover)
    1. Saltwater fly fishing. I. Title.
    SH456.2 .S73 2002
    799.1'6—dc21

                                            2002007803

CONTENTS

ACKNOWLEDGMENTS

TO MY FATHER who gave me my first rod and took me on my first fishing trip, winter flounder fishing on Long Island Sound. It wasn't fly fishing, but it was fishing on the salt and it did put the passion in my heart and very soul. From that moment on, I could never experience enough fishing to satisfy the urge. Thanks for getting me hooked Dad.

To Bill Adams for teaching me how to tie my first fly, a Gold Ribbed Hare's Ear. It was a great lesson and you would be amazed how far it took me. Thanks for sharing your skills.

To Frank Rhode for putting the first piece of cane in my hands and for showing me the ways of the trout on those fabled trout waters of the Catskills. I was already hooked on fishing, now I was addicted to fly fishing. Thanks Frank.

Thanks, to all those skinny water guides that shared their fishing holes and expertise with me.

To Peter "Van" Gytenbeek for giving me my first writing break with *Fly Fishing in Saltwaters.* Thanks Van.

Warm thanks to Greg and Carol Mentzer, one of the top fly fishing couples in the sport today, for their wonderful friendship and frequent companionship on those chilly salty mornings. We met on the water for the first time . . . hopefully we will share many more days of fair weather, bountiful seas and bent rods. I am especially grateful to Greg for his editorial and technical assistance and for providing some great images for the book. A better Montana trout guide you will not find. Thanks Montana Man!!!

To David Richie, Editor *Fly Fishing in Saltwaters,* for continuing to support my writing. Thanks to you David, and your talented staff for producing such a wonderful publication.

I am especially indebted to a special friend of mine, Rick Bender, an exceptional fly fisherman, fly tier and newly re-discovered artist who shared his talent, expertise and time and in no small way contributed to the preparation of this book. We have shared many of the endless spectacles that nature has to offer on the salty seas and I cease to be amazed at his innate ability to see natures details that few of us ever realize, let alone appreciate. Thanks Rick!

To Peter Burford, of Burford Books, for believing in me. Thanks Peter for making the book a reality.

FOREWORD

Saltwater Fly Fishing: Seven Strategies for Success is an excellent work. Many books today are written by anglers with limited exposure to the sport of fly fishing. Mike Starke has spent a lifetime gathering the advice contained in this book. He has taken a practical and different approach by listing seven strategies that are the basis of effectively fly fishing the salt.

This book covers every area, from learning about tides to how to present a well-cast fly. Weather, evaluating when and where to fish, and choosing the correct flies, the right tackle and other important factors are all covered in great detail. Presentation is the most important factor in catching any fish and Mike does a masterful job of outlining how to accomplish this.

This is a book written by a true fly fisherman and it will benefit both the angler just getting into the sport and anyone who has spent years chasing saltwater species. I highly recommend it.

—Lefty Kreh

INTRODUCTION

Ten percent of fishermen catch 90 percent of the fish. I don't know who said it first, but this statement is remarkably accurate, especially for saltwater fly fishing. Contrary to many fresh waters that fly fishermen can slip into with the confidence of putting on a familiar and comfortable pair of jeans, salt waters are often overwhelming and downright intimidating to novices and experienced anglers alike. Oceans and estuaries are vast open bodies of water that are subjected to the constantly changing effects of wind, waves, tide, and temperature. But where and how does a fly angler begin mastery of such a challenging, yet exciting fly-fishing arena? Just like the oceans themselves, the vastness of learning to fly fish in salt waters can also be overwhelming and intimidating.

There's so much information out there! Where do I start? What do I need to know and do? How can I learn and develop my skills? How can I be more successful? There are seemingly so many things to learn that many people tend to get overwhelmed. New fly fishermen want to attain some immediate success, while experienced ones want to achieve greater success. In the process of trying to learn everything, many get lost in the detail. This approach is very tactical, and overall success will be limited. To the contrary, people tend to learn more by understanding major concepts, themes, or what I call . . . strategies.

The purpose of this book is to identify and describe what I believe are the seven strategies that enable anglers to be successful fly fishing in salt

7

waters. These seven strategies are essentially what you need to *do* to be successful. The book not only covers the "how to's" of the core strategies such as becoming a proficient caster, spending time on the water, using the right fly, maximizing your presentation, and hooking up and staying hooked, but also explains and provides examples of "why" these strategies are so important to different fishing situations. I also tried to review these strategies differently to give a fresh perspective and hopefully some new insight to experienced fly anglers. The other key strategies—learning continuously and planning your fishing—are rarely written about, yet they are so important for success.

These seven strategies and their tactics apply to shore/wade fishing and boat fishing alike. By understanding and practicing these seven strategies, you'll be able to apply what you've learned and the skills you develop to virtually any species of fish and to just about any fishing situation to increase your success.

—Mike Starke

STRATEGY

LEARN CONTINUOUSLY

THE AWAKENING

I've been fly fishing for over 35 years and like most saltwater fly fishermen, my roots were in freshwater fly fishing. As a teenager in the late 1960s and early 1970s, I was fortunate to have fished the fabled Catskill trout waters that included the Esopus, Willowemoc, and Big Beaverkill. These were wonderful and highly productive trout waters. Although certainly not as big as western rivers, these eastern streams were fairly wide and susceptible to windy conditions, which made fly casting a challenge even for the experienced angler.

Years later, after getting married and raising children, I began to explore saltwater fly fishing while on vacation in Florida. Like many, I was fascinated by the shallow flats fishing for exotic species like bonefish, tarpon, and . . . "snook and redfish." I thought it would be a thrill to go after them with the fly rod. After all, I was a pretty fair fly fisherman . . . I could cast 60 feet or more while fishing for trout . . . piece of cake (or so I thought). The one intelligent thing I did was book a professional guide who knew the waters and was an accomplished fly fisherman with all the necessary tackle.

Early in the morning, we left from Islamorada and headed into the backcountry of Florida Bay in search of redfish, snook, or tarpon on the fly. Needless to say, I was pumped up with anticipation of getting my first saltwater fish on the fly. We approached a small mangrove island, and the guide shut the motor down and began poling us closer to shore. I assumed the position on the bow and stripped out an ambitious pile of line on the deck. After just a few minutes, the guide said, "Eleven o'clock. A few nice snook coming down the shore toward us. Go ahead and cast." Well, easier said than done. Those snook seemed awfully far away . . . about 70 feet. Still, with all that adrenaline pumping, I never thought I couldn't make the cast.

With great excitement, I began to make my false casts and feed line in order to reach the distant target. One false cast, two false casts, three false casts, four false . . . you get the picture. "What are you doing?" said the guide. "Shoot the line! Shoot it!" Up to this point I thought I was doing pretty good; now my confidence level went way down. I made a couple more false casts to try to get all the necessary line out to reach the target. I was rapidly losing control of the fly line when I finally fired away. The snook were long gone before my fly even touched the water—not that it was even remotely close to its intended target anyway.

My guide, obviously very disappointed with my performance, began to give advice in a foreign language. He was apparently explaining what I should have done. He mentioned something about making as few false casts as possible, double hauling, and then shooting the line and fly to the target. In a confused state, I turned to him and asked, "What's a double haul and how the hell do you shoot line?" My guide was patient. He realized I was like a fish out of water when it came to casting in salt water. He offered me suggestions and gave me a quick on-the-water casting lesson to enable me to catch a few nice redfish. I was very grateful.

My guide gave me some very important advice. He told me that to be successful at saltwater fly fishing, you need to learn as much as you can and practice what you learn so that when you do go fishing, you'll be more successful and have a much more enjoyable experience. That advice, my friends, was not free. It cost $350 plus tip, but looking back, I'd have to say it was worth every penny.

That day was truly a humbling experience. After that day, I vowed never to be caught so unprepared again, and I committed myself to learning continuously about saltwater fly fishing so I could be more successful, continue to develop, and, yes, learn to spend my money more wisely.

That fishing experience was an awakening, and it led to a profound change—an extremely positive change. *If you continue to do what you've always done, you'll always get what you always got.* Boy, what a great saying. I wish I could take credit for coming up with it. I realized that if I was ever to become more successful at saltwater fly fishing, I had to begin to do things differently. From that early experience, I found out that I hardly knew anything about saltwater fly fishing and certainly did not have the casting skills that are critical to the sport. Rather than feeling down, I felt energized. I wanted to and knew I had to learn everything I possibly could about saltwater fly fishing in order to become significantly more successful. I was excited about the possibilities and up for the challenge.

As soon as I arrived home, I began to read everything I could get my hands on that had to do with saltwater fly fishing. The more I learned, the more I wanted to learn. I soon discovered that there were many different ways to gain knowledge and develop skills. Too bad I didn't do it before going fishing. The following are just some of the ways that you can learn continuously to increase your saltwater fly-fishing knowledge and skill level. I can already hear some of the excuses now: I'm too busy, I don't have the time, yada, yada, yada. Anything worth having is worth planning and working for. Choose a special time of day to spend time learning about saltwater fly fishing, even if it's just 15 minutes a day. The important thing is, you have to plan and get in the habit of spending the time. Otherwise you'll probably never do it.

READ

The first and perhaps easiest ways to learn is by reading. For this section, I'm going to limit our discussion to printed stuff; I'll turn to the Web later on.

When it finally dawned on me that I needed to learn, I went and searched bookstores and even tackle shops for magazines that had saltwater fly fishing as their primary focus. There's a comprehensive list of magazines in the references at the end of this book to help you select the ones most appropriate for your use. My two favorites are *Fly Fishing in Salt Waters* and *Saltwater Fly Fishing*. These are two world-class magazines, both in the quality of their articles and the photography/graphics. They're both published on a bimonthly basis. They're chock-full of information all about nothing but saltwater fly fishing, including fishing destinations (both local and exotic), budget fishing, species-specific fishing tips (stripers, bonefish), area-specific fishing tips (Cape Cod, southwest Florida), fly tying, rods and reels, gear, and more. There are several other fine fly-fishing magazines that do include articles on saltwater fly fishing, but only these two are entirely dedicated to the sport. You can also find local fishing magazines that cover specific areas, techniques, and species.

There is a wide variety of books available on the subject of saltwater fly fishing. Some books cover the technical aspects of saltwater fishing from A to Z, while others cover more specific locales or concentrate on a particular gamefish. No fly-fishing library would be complete without several books by the legendary Bernard "Lefty" Kreh. Lefty's book *Fly Fishing in Salt Water* is an outstanding source of information for the novice and expert angler alike. It was my first fly-fishing book. Other fine books such as Lou Tabory's *Inshore Fly Fishing* and Tom Earnhardt's *Fly Fishing the Tidewaters* are excellent sources of information, especially if you fly fish the salt along the East Coast. If you're planning to target a certain species on an upcoming trip, there's a good chance that an author has written a book about it. What better way to prepare than to learn about that fish's habits and the tackle and tactics necessary to be successful? Randall Kaufmann's book *Bonefishing with a Fly* proved an invaluable tool that enabled me to hone my bonefishing skills. If you're going to fish a particular area, chances are there's a fly-fishing book that covers it. These books are excellent sources of information for where and when to go, where to stay, hot fishing spots, what gamefish are likely to be encountered, and so forth.

Besides learning, an added benefit to reading is that it's a great escape. You can enjoy yourself and reduce that pent-up stress without even leaving the comfort of your own home.

WATCH VIDEOTAPES

There is a wide assortment of videotapes available on the market today. They cover a multitude of subjects that include rod building, casting, fly tying, and fly fishing for a wide range of saltwater species. Videos can be a good source of information. However, videos are especially worthwhile when they illustrate how to do a particular task or movement (fly tying, double hauling). They can also be very beneficial in treating cabin fever when you're unable to go fishing, or take you to far-off destinations that you may one day plan to fish . . . or at least dream about.

SURF THE WEB

With the advent of the Internet, learning has never been easier, quicker, or more readily available. A few clicks here and a few clicks there, and you can access almost any information imaginable. Fly-fishing information is no exception. Currently, there are numerous fly-fishing Web sites that contain links to everything from the latest gear and tackle to flies and hot spots around the globe. It's astonishing! Perhaps some of the most useful and practical information available via the Web includes tidal information, weather reports, and general fishing information that can be gleaned from the infamous message boards.

If you fish the salt, you'll need to be concerned with the tides and weather, more so if you're fishing near-shore waters. I fish primarily from an 18-foot center console and cover everything from the back bays to near-shore fishing along the mid-Atlantic coast. As such, I must be concerned with my personal safety and the safety of my guests and clients. Weather forecasts and water conditions are critical to planning each trip. Before deciding where and when to fish, I access a Web site like Tide Predictor to find out what locations will have the most favorable tides. If I'm planning to fish, say, the Turks and Caicos in the Bahamas, I can determine the optimum time to be there and plan my trip accordingly.

Regarding weather, a few clicks at my favorite Web sites and I have the latest forecast of air and sea temperatures, wind speed and direction, visibility, and precipitation. Since weather often affects fishing conditions and is critical for boat- and surf-fisherman safety, I usually check a variety of weather Web sites. One of my favorites is www.wunderground.com, which gives me a five-day forecast and includes a marine forecast as well. These two forecasts are usually sufficient to give me an idea of the expected weather conditions for fishing in more protected waters like the Chesapeake Bay. However, if I plan to fish near-shore waters along the coast, I also need to get the ocean conditions.

The U.S. Oceanographic Institute has numerous ocean buoys located all along the U.S. coasts and in various bays. You can locate these buoys at www.Offshoreweather.com. If, for example, I was planning to fish along Jersey's southern coast, I would bookmark and access the Delaware Bay Buoy located some 20 miles east of Ocean City, Maryland. These buoys provide some fantastic up-to-the-minute information on the weather and ocean surface conditions. From this buoy, I can get the current air and surface water temperature, wind speed and direction, and wave and swell height and steepness. This is incredibly valuable information that is readily available 24 hours a day, seven day a week. It is sure to help you plan a safe and successful fishing trip.

When surfing the Net, you need to use your time wisely. It's easy to lose track of time. Message boards can be very helpful, but can also be frustrating and a waste of time. Accessing local Web sites to find information can be useful in your planning. Folks will often post fishing reports on local waters. Some may be rather general—"the fish are in and here's what we caught them on." Other folks post fishing reports in mind-blowing detail. These can include the times, tides, fish caught, weights/lengths, flies that worked, lines and leaders used, type of rod and reel, and so on, and so on. You get the picture. The trick is that you must be wise in extracting the useful information. Many of these reports do not contain very useful information. If you're not careful, you can find yourself lost in the abyss of minutiae. On the other hand, you can often find very helpful stuff that can lead you to a successful trip. Case in point—my fishing buddy Greg Mentzer and I were looking to do some late-fall fishing in the Chesapeake. Greg was scanning the one of our favorite Web sites, www.tidalfish.com (formally worldwideangler.com), and noticed a report regarding fish off Bloody Point Light in the middle Chesapeake Bay. It was also supported by a few other related posts that led us to believe it was accurate. The next day we went fishing at Bloody Point Light and had an excellent day.

My best advice regarding fishing reports or posts on message boards is to try to find other supporting information on the same Web site or others. If you notice a number of other people posting similar fishing reports for the same area, the chances are good that they are reliable. However, remember that fishing is fishing, and conditions do and will change suddenly.

I also suggest visiting not only the larger and more popular Web sites, but also some of the smaller private sites as well. Many guides, for example (including myself), have Web sites and will include current fishing reports. Some of these smaller Web sites can be like finding a pot of gold. Often they are updated more frequently then the larger sites, especially when the fishing gets hot.

Find the Web sites that provide the most enjoyment and benefit to you. Bookmark these for future reference. Time will tell you which reports are most accurate. Stick with these to increase your odds of success. Of course fishing is great, but surfing around a bit is good, too. You never know what gems you might find.

NETWORK

No man is an island. Nobody is born having all the knowledge about all things. While learning to be more successful at fly fishing, we can choose to take the difficult path or the path of least resistance. We can take the challenge to the extreme and feel we have not truly learned to be successful unless we have been entirely self-taught . . . or we can speed up the learning process and try to make it as painless as possible by learning from others who have already traveled the path.

I have known all too many fly fishermen and have seen way too many Internet posts on various Web sites from folks who would sooner die than ask for help from a fellow fly fisherman on how to improve their casting. Sure, they get some printed information on trying this technique or that technique, but they seem to have an unwarranted fear of asking a real live person to show them how to actually do it. Perhaps it's fear of rejection, or maybe it's an ego thing. I really don't know. I do know this, however: If you have not solicited or taken advantage of a helping hand from a fellow angler, you are short-circuiting your learning process and have missed out on one hell of an opportunity.

To "network" is to have opportunities to learn and develop through collaborative interactions with others. Hopefully, you have also experienced the great willingness of many fellow anglers to share experiences about how to tie flies, build rods, cast, and perhaps even the secrets of finding those big ones. Life is too short to waste time. I believe you can learn and become more successful faster if you surround yourself with friends, acquaintances, fishing buddies, and other folks who are able and willing to share with you what they know.

One of the best ways to get a network going is to join a local fly-fishing club or start your own. The members of these clubs can often be a wonderful source of information, and there always seems to be an open hand willing to show you the way. Are all these folks experts? No, many are not, but everyone usually has something to offer you, even if it's their friendship. With networking, you can acquire more in-depth knowledge about a subject or skill, or broaden your experiences. You may learn more about techniques for fishing for a certain species or you may simply learn patience and a deeper appreciation for the outdoors. The learning process is often more productive and more enjoyable when networking with other folks who share the same passion for fly fishing as yourself. Any way you look at it, you come out a winner.

South Jersey Fly Fishers Club outing on the Chesapeake Bay. (L-R; Author, John Waters, Bruce Mitchell and Bob Shaffer) Joining and participating in a fly-fishing club is a great way to network.

Here are some suggestions on getting started with your fly-fishing network:

- Get to know as many different saltwater fly fishermen as possible—*more* is the operative word. The more people you know, the more possibilities for learning.
- Join a fly-fishing club to meet new folks (salt water, if possible).
- Develop long-distance relationships with fellow fly-fishing Web surfers.
- Seek out other people at work who fly fish.
- Volunteer to participate in your club events and shows.
- Get to know other anglers while out fishing. I met one of my best friends while fly fishing on the Chesapeake Bay. I meet countless others at marinas or walking the beaches.
- Take a fly-tying or -casting lesson.
- Be willing to share what you know with others. You will be paid back tenfold.

ADOPT A MENTOR

Adopting a mentor in its purest sense would be finding someone who is more knowledgeable, skilled, and/or experienced than yourself and is willing to coach you or take you under his wing to share his knowledge and skills with you. In some instances you might wish to be mentored by someone, but he's just unavailable or unwilling to mentor you. That being the case, it's still okay to try to learn from or mimic that person as much as you can without him being an "official" mentor. It's also important to have more than just one mentor; have several, and between them you'll learn a ton.

Example of mentors might include:

- A friend or relative.
- An acquaintance or friend from a fishing club.
- A well-known fishing personality (Lefty Kreh, Flip Pallot).
- A fellow Internet surfer.
- Someone with skill sets different than yours.

Besides finding someone who is willing to mentor you, you want to choose fly fishermen who have either more knowledge or a more highly developed skill set than yourself. For example, I had just taken a new job and moved to southern New Jersey. I was somewhat familiar with the Jersey shore and Delaware Bay, but hadn't even thought of fly fishing the Chesapeake Bay.

During a meeting of the South Jersey Fly Fishers, I overheard a fellow club member, John Waters, mention something about catching stripers in the Chesapeake Bay. Being inquisitive, I questioned John a bit about his fishing experience on the Chesapeake and told him that I would love to learn more about where to fish. As it turned out, John is a super guy and always willing to help out a fellow angler. His enthusiasm is quite contagious.

The author providing a student from Greg Mentzer's Fly Fishing School with a lesson in casting. (Photo: Greg and Carol Mentzer)

Before we even finished our conversation, John had planned a trip the following week with a few other club members.

A short time later I was fishing the Chesapeake. We had a fabulous time catching stripers on the fly. I just couldn't believe that for several years while living in southern Jersey, I was within just a one- or two-hour drive of the upper and middle Chesapeake. Talk about being mentally blocked! My friendship with John opened the door to the wonderful fishing of the beautiful Chesapeake. God only made one Chesapeake Bay . . . I thank John Waters for showing me the way.

Here are just some examples of what you might be able to learn from mentors:
- Choosing the right rod and reel.
- How to fly cast as a beginner, intermediate, or advanced caster.
- What knots should be used and how to tie them properly.
- How to tie flies as a beginner, intermediate, or advanced tier.
- Where the generally best places are to fish from shore or boat.
- How to appreciate the sunrises and sunsets.
- Rod-building techniques.
- How to select the right fly for different situations.
- When is the best time to target different species.
- How to be patient in tough fishing situations.
- What to bring and wear when fishing the surf.
- Where the best places are to eat.
- How to handle a boat properly and safely in different situations.
- Where some secret honey holes are (if you're lucky).
- How to share your knowledge with others.

Your understanding of fly fishing will be greatly enhanced by adopting mentors who have more knowledge/skills than you. If you don't know how to cast or tie flies, adopt a mentor who does. He doesn't have to be the best caster or tier in the world for you to learn. Once you feel you've been a good sponge and have learned his techniques, find another mentor who has more highly developed skills and repeat the process. By having many mentors with different skills and knowledge and different levels of them, you can learn and develop skills at an astonishing rate. By applying these new skills and knowledge, you will observe that you are also becoming more successful at fly fishing.

USE GUIDES

Using the services of professional fly-fishing guides when fishing a new area, especially with limited time, is invaluable. Learning the water to be successful takes time—time you may not have or be willing to spend.

Buying the services of a guide just might not fit the budgets of some folks. That's okay. However, many folks who could afford to hire a guide choose not to. This is okay, too, if you don't mind just taking a boat ride. Salt water usually means *big* water, and water that is productive only at certain times of day, year, and/or tide. Knowing when and where to fish and what species to target is dependent to a large extent on local knowledge of the waters and the angler's experience. When you hire a guide, that's what you're paying for. That knowledge and experience come at a price. A guided charter for a full day (approximately eight hours) can range anywhere from $300 to $500 plus tip. If you have a fishing partner to share expenses you can cut the price in half for each angler, which just may make it affordable.

The true value of using a guide is realized time and time again. Spending $300 or so on a one-day guided trip may seem so outrageously expensive that many anglers won't even consider using one, even though they probably could well afford it. Fishing time is precious. Catching time is priceless. Now, don't misunderstand me. I've spent many a day fishing and not catching, with no regrets and feeling downright privileged to be fortunate enough to have spent the day relaxing on the water and perhaps enjoying the company of a friend. But remember, I do my research, have the right tackle, and understand the habits of the fish I am targeting. For various reasons, there are days when I'm just not able to catch fish. That happens from time to time, especially when fishing large expansive saltwaters. There's a big difference between this and those anglers who really don't have intimate knowledge of the fishing situation that they're pursuing. They'll go week after week and sometimes year after year spending hundreds, if not thousands of dollars in pursuit of their passion. Sure, they have tons of enthusiasm, but that doesn't necessarily translate into fish on the end of their lines. What they often lack is practical knowledge, which is exactly what a good guide can give them to increase their odds of catching fish.

When I'm paying for a guide I like to get my money's worth, so I ask a fair amount of questions throughout the day. Every guide is different, so test the waters first with some general questions. Over the course of the day, ask pertinent questions as situations present themselves. Most of the guides I have used have been very cordial and willing to share a great deal of information if you show an interest and are not overburdensome. When I was sight fishing for redfish and snook in the Ten Thousand Island area of southwest Florida years back, I asked my guide, Jim Nickerson, how he knew which cove would be more productive than another. They all looked alike to me. He shared a great tip for locating fish by telling me he looks to see if there are any wading birds in the water actively feeding. If so, there are probably baitfish around. And of course, where there are baitfish, there are usually predatory fish as well. He was right! A great tip to remember.

The following are examples of questions that should be asked of guides. Some of these may even be asked before booking the trip. How guides answer the questions will give you a good idea whether they're qualified and the best time to book the trip. This will optimize your chances of success. This information will also help you prepare your equipment, gear, and flies for the trip.

- What types of fishing opportunities are available in winter (spring, summer, fall)?
- What types of fish would we be targeting (snook, bonefish, stripers, false albacore)?
- Where would we be fishing (mudflats, along mangrove shoreline in the backcountry, along the beaches, offshore)?
- What type of boat do you have and why do you prefer that type?
- What rod-and-reel setup is needed?
- What depths will the fish be at and what type of fly lines work best?
- What flies are most productive (colors, sizes, weighted, flash)?
- What are the most effective retrieves?
- What tide is best—incoming or outgoing?
- What leader setup do you recommend?
- What kind of gear do you suggest I bring?

Spending a day with a qualified guide even on your local waters can expose you to great fishing experiences you didn't think were possible. It can also open the door to a wealth of newfound knowledge that can benefit you time and time again in increasing your angling success.

STRATEGY 1—LEARN CONTINUOUSLY

Enhance your understanding and enjoyment of saltwater fly fishing by...

- Reading books, magazines, newspaper articles, club newsletters.
- Watching videos to learn information and help develop skills.
- Surfing the Web to find out almost anything you want to know about saltwater fly fishing.
- Networking with others to develop collaborative interactions and enhance learning.
- Adopting mentors who set an example to follow and/or who can help coach you.
- Using guides. They can put you onto fish and accelerate your learning.

STRATEGY 2

BECOME A PROFICIENT CASTER

L et's face it, fly casting is the foundation of fly fishing. If a single factor makes the difference between catching fish and not catching fish in salt water, it's probably the angler's ability to cast proficiently. In saltwater fly fishing, casting is many anglers' Achilles' heel.

For most saltwater fly fishermen, including myself, our roots are in fishing freshwater rivers, streams, and creeks. In many of these fishing environments, anglers need only cast a fly an average distance of 30 feet to

INEFFECTIVE CASTING

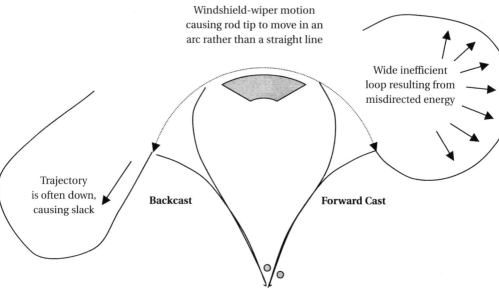

Windshield-wiper motion causing rod tip to move in an arc rather than a straight line

Wide inefficient loop resulting from misdirected energy

Trajectory is often down, causing slack

Backcast

Forward Cast

THE BASIC CASTING STROKE

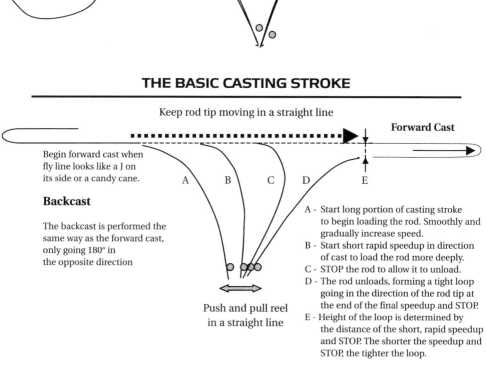

Keep rod tip moving in a straight line

Forward Cast

Begin forward cast when fly line looks like a J on its side or a candy cane.

A   B   C   D   E

Backcast

The backcast is performed the same way as the forward cast, only going 180° in the opposite direction

Push and pull reel in a straight line

A - Start long portion of casting stroke to begin loading the rod. Smoothly and gradually increase speed.
B - Start short rapid speedup in direction of cast to load the rod more deeply.
C - STOP the rod to allow it to unload.
D - The rod unloads, forming a tight loop going in the direction of the rod tip at the end of the final speedup and STOP.
E - Height of the loop is determined by the distance of the short, rapid speedup and STOP. The shorter the speedup and STOP, the tighter the loop.

catch fish on a regular basis. Being a proficient caster in these situations is important, but it's not critical. Even with big wide casting loops, an un-skilled angler can often cast and catch fish in fresh water. This is probably the main reason why many anglers never really learn to fly cast correctly. Heck, I ought to know . . . I was one of them for a while.

In most saltwater fly-fishing situations, anglers cannot hide from the ef-fects of the wind or the challenges that longer distances, heavier equip-ment, and larger flies will create. You won't be able to hide your lack of casting proficiency. Any casting flaw will be greatly magnified fly fishing the salt. If you apply yourself and take some time to learn how to cast with proficiency, you'll be a much improved fisherman in both salt and fresh waters.

THE MECHANICS

A sound understanding of fly-casting mechanics is critical to the saltwater fly fisherman. Everything else learned in fly casting—accuracy, distance— is built upon this foundation of understanding. Not learning the proper mechanics of casting and expecting to be successful fly fishing the salt is like trying to write a novel without first having learned your ABCs. It just won't work. It's that simple.

Still, just because the mechanics of fly casting are critical doesn't mean they have to be difficult to learn. Practice alone will not make you a profi-cient caster. You need to practice the correct mechanics of casting correctly. In fact, practicing and fishing while using improper technique is quite destructive in that you will develop muscle memory and habits that are incorrect and ineffective.

Casting correctly starts with understanding a little about the physics of making a cast. First, the fly rod is nothing more than a long, flexible lever that is designed to stay *straight* when at rest. When we put the rod into mo-tion during a cast, we are essentially forcing the rod into a bend (loading) and then back into a straight position (unloading). A fly rod in a bent po-sition has stored energy. The bigger the bend we force into the rod during the cast, the more energy is stored. A short casting motion or stroke will put a slight bend in the rod. A long casting motion or stroke will put a larger bend in the rod. When the bent rod is stopped on the forward or backcast, the stored energy in the rod is transferred to the fly line in the form of a loop that enables us to cast a fly. To make a short cast, an angler

Rick Bender gives an impromptu demonstration of a medium-distance casting sequence. Notice the good extension on the backcast with the rod drifting back and fly line almost straightened out in preparation for a smooth transition to the forward cast.

The forward cast is made. Towards the end of the cut there is a very short speedup and haul to load the rod fully.

The rod is *stopped*, allowing the rod to unload.

A tight loop with a high degree of line speed is formed.

The tight loop quickly extends, allowing Rick to shoot line to a distant target, even in windy conditions.

only needs to put a slight bend in the rod tip with a short casting stroke. A long cast requires a deep bend extending down to the butt section of the rod, which is accomplished with a long casting stroke.

It's very important to note that during each casting stroke, the rod must continue to be accelerated smoothly in order to develop and maintain the bend or load in the rod. At the very end of each casting stroke there needs to be a very short, rapid speedup and *stop*. This short, rapid speedup and *stop* is critical in maximizing the bend or load of the rod and transferring the rod's stored energy to the fly line to form the loop and make the cast. The shorter the speedup and the quicker the *stop* at the end of the cast, the tighter the loop and the farther the cast. The *stop* at the end of each casting stroke is extremely important for forming the tight casting loops that make for effective and efficient fly casting. A not-so-quick *stoooop* at the end of the cast will form a wider or open casting loop that won't have the velocity to travel very far. A quick, definitive *stop* at the end of the cast will form a much tighter casting loop with greater velocity to travel greater distances. This is basic casting physics in a nutshell. Enough said.

Before discussing the key elements of casting, I'd like to emphasize that for the most part, proper fly casting has absolutely nothing to do with arcs. Proper fly casting is primarily about straight lines. Most dated fly-casting books and some folks even today still refer to casting in terms of arcs. In my opinion this image of casting arcs is totally incorrect. It's probably the biggest obstacle to learning proper casting technique and has been and continues to be used to the detriment of many anglers. The classic "windshield-wiper style" or casting arc that many freshwater and some saltwater anglers use is for all intents and purposes useless for fly fishing in salt water. It is a very ineffective and inefficient way of fly casting. Instead of focusing the energy of the cast toward the target like an arrow, the windshield-wiper style cast spreads the energy around an arc and dilutes its power and effectiveness.

When faced with covering greater distances with a fly in winds that generally average 10 to 15 mph, fly casting in saltwater conditions requires sound principles and skills to be both effective and efficient. In my experience, *Lefty Kreh's Modern Fly Casting Method* is unquestionably the best fly-casting method to use when fly fishing in salt waters. Lefty's casting method is described in detail in both *Lefty's Little Library of Fly Fishing,* published by Odysseus Editions, and *Presenting the Fly* published by The Lyons Press. Aside from being very effective, I find Lefty's casting method to be very efficient. Little energy is wasted, and casting is accomplished in a natural and relaxed position. This is essential when you may be blind casting large flies long distances hundreds of time in a single day. The windshield-wiper, karate-chop, ten-o'clock-to-one-o'clock styles of casting are very ineffective in these situations. I know all too many people both young and old who complain of elbow and shoulder aches and pains because they use these styles.

This is probably as good a place as any to talk a little about rods and what action is best. Even though you may be an excellent caster, you won't be able to cast well in saltwater conditions without the proper tool, in this case the right rod that has the "right" action. To cast effectively and efficiently in salt waters I highly recommend using 9–9 ½ foot fly rods that are stiffer and have a fast-action, or what is often referred to as a tip-flex. The reasons are two-fold; 1) a stiffer/faster-tip action will permit you to make quicker and longer casts more effectively and efficiently, and 2) a stiffer rod has more backbone for fighting and lifting big fish.

There are variations from rod manufacturer to rod manufacturer and rod model to rod model. Most important are the angler's personal preferences. The best way to find out what specific rod fits your casting style is to visit a professional fly shop to seek advice. Keep in mind that if you over-line some rods with one-weight-heavier fly line, you can often enhance the rod's performance. I often over-line my fly rods to increase the load of the rod, which gives me the ability to cast quickly and make long cast all day long with minimum effort. But what suits me may not suit you. Do your experimentation at the fly shop *before* you commit.

While I don't wish to reiterate the details of Lefty's casting principles, I'd like to share with you my own thoughts regarding some simple techniques that may improve your casting. As I mentioned previously, proper fly casting is all about *straight* lines, not arcs. This involves a straight rhythmic push–pull motion with your upper arm relaxed down along your side and your forearm tilted outward slightly at about a 45-degree angle from your body. Keeping your arm relaxed at your side is very important in maintaining a natural back-and-forth or push–pull sawing motion that will not overtire and overstress the shoulder or elbow muscles and joints.

If you were to take hold of a half-full plastic 1-gallon container (about 4 pounds) as you would your rod, and raise it until your elbow was almost at the same height as your shoulder, you would find that this would put considerable stress and strain on your shoulder muscles and joints. Now, if you were to move your forearm back and forth in the classic windshield-washer/karate-chop style, you would have excessive stress and strain on your elbow and even more on your shoulder. Remember, a 9- or 10-weight outfit weighs considerably more than a 4- or 5-weight outfit. Can you imagine how stressful and painful it would be to hold your arm in that position for four to six hours a day, let alone making hundreds, if not thousands, of casts? I can! No wonder so many fly casters have sore shoulders and elbows.

The push–pull sawing/casting motion that I am recommending allows you to keep your upper casting arm relaxed at your side and your elbow low, thereby reducing stress and strain on muscles and joints. This will enable you to cast with heavier rods, reels, lines, and flies for hours on end without fatigue. Performing the entire cast in a smooth rhythmic motion— starting off slowly, gradually building rod speed and load, and speeding up and stopping at the end of the stroke—will greatly increase your casting effectiveness while making the experience much more enjoyable. A practical thing to keep in mind is that lengthening the entire casting stroke with the rod makes it easier not only to make longer casts, but also to cast into the wind and/or cast those heavier flies.

Here's some more *straight* talk:
1. Align your thumb *straight* on top of the rod.
2. Keep your wrist *straight*. Do not bend it on the forward or backcasts.
3. Point your rod tip down and make sure your fly line is *straight* before attempting to cast to remove any slack.
4. Make your backcast by pulling *straight* back on a slight upward angle 180 degrees from the target.
5. Wait until the line is almost *straight* before pushing or pulling on your forward or backcast.
6. Throughout the casting stroke, keep your hand and rod tip moving in a *straight* line.
7. To cast the fly, make a short, rapid speedup and *stop* and point the rod tip *straight* at the target at about eye level.

Note: If you don't have a qualified friend or instructor, try using a video recorder as an aid to help you learn proper casting techniques.

ACCURACY

In my early fly-fishing days I was a dry-fly diehard and fished throughout the Catskill Mountains, especially on the Beaverkill. Casting accuracy was important, but it wasn't critical in most situations. If the fly didn't quite land where I wanted it to the first time, I often had a second, third, or more chances to deliver it to the target. You see, those trout lived right there in that pool or riffle. They weren't going anywhere. If I didn't catch them I could come back later, tomorrow or next week, and there would be a good chance that they would still be rising in the same pool taking dry flies.

Years later I began fly fishing salt waters in Florida, the Bahamas, and the Caribbean when on vacation. My fly-fishing adventures in the Tropics primarily included sight fishing for snook, redfish, and bonefish. What I quickly learned when pursuing these species in shallow waters was that casting accuracy was not just important, it was critical. When fishing for skinny-water species such as bonefish and redfish, precision casts are an absolute must in many situations. Unlike trout in a river pool, if your cast is not right on target for these shallow-water species, you will probably never have another opportunity to catch those fish again. They'll be gone forever.

Casting along the shadows of mangrove edges.

Fly fishing in the backcountry of the Everglades offers its own casting challenges. Here, you often need to place your fly along the very edges and in small openings of the mangroves where snook wait to ambush prey or where they, along with redfish and tarpon, cruise the edges looking for an easy meal. If your cast isn't within inches of the mangroves, you'll often fail to entice a strike, and if your cast goes a little too far you'll have to go hunting for your fly in the mangrove branches.

When fly fishing from the surf or a boat for species such as striped bass, bluefish, speckled/gray trout, and false albacore, very accurate casting is often not a necessity. Anglers for the most part are blind casting to likely fish-holding locations with the hope that if they cover enough water, their fly will eventually cross the path of a fish. Casting distance is probably more important than accuracy, since the fish are most often not visible to the angler. Still, that's not to say that anglers shouldn't be capable of casting accurately when the situation calls for it. They should be.

To cast accurately, you need to constantly remember to use good technique as described previously, and that the end of the line and the fly will go in the same direction as the rod tip at the very end of the forward or backcast. It's that simple. However, many casters don't really pay attention to the direction of the rod tip at the end of their casts. Many casters think that they make a quick speedup and *stop* and point the rod tip to the target, but usually don't. They dip or twist their wrist at the end of the cast, which results in a wide-open casting loop, causing the line and fly to crash into the water short of the target or else to go to one side or the other. For accurate casts, use good technique, don't bend or twist your wrist, and make a short, rapid speedup and *stop,* being sure to point the rod tip *straight* at the target generally about eye-level high. As always, start with a short line and practice until you're proficient before casting more line.

Sight-fishing opportunities may present themselves when species of fish like striped bass, bluefish, trout, or false albacore feed at the surface or indicate their presence with nervous water or boils. Often, these opportunities are short-lived. If an angler cannot present the fly accurately to the target, the opportunity may be lost. Case in point: I was out spring striper fishing on the upper Chesapeake Bay with a friend. It was first light and we had just gone about 1 mile south of the marina when I noticed some bird activity. Idling down the motor and approaching the area quietly, we noticed several surface boils and an occasional eruption as stripers fed on

Author with a nice snook taken tight along a mangrove edge. Casting accuracy is often critical for success.

white perch about 6 to 8 inches below the surface. Stunned perch were floating to or near the surface, where after a few death-twitches they would disappear into the maw of a hungry striper.

We grabbed our rods, stripped out line, and began blind casting in the areas where we saw the boils. No takers. We continued to blind cast; then there was a nice boil 50 to 60 feet off the side of the boat. Quickly picking up my line, I shot a cast directly to the boil. I let the fly settle a bit, gave it a slight twitch, and the line came tight with a nice plump 16-pound striper. After releasing the first fish, I waited with the fly between my fingers for an-other rise or boil to cast to. The surface boils were only spotty. There didn't appear to be many stripers by the looks of my fish finder—just a nice one here and there. When a fish would show itself with a boil or a gulp, an ac-curate cast to the area usually brought a strike. Our unexpected luck lasted only about 45 minutes, but I managed to catch and release a dozen nice stripers (or rocks, as they're called in the Chesapeake) between 10 and 16 pounds. A very good start for the day. Oh yes . . . my friend—who is a very good trout fisherman and occasionally fly fishes the salt—was not prepared for what happened and managed only a few stripers. *Frustration* would not accurately describe his state. He had difficulty getting his fly to the boils and was for all intents and purposes just blind casting. With a limited number of stripers in the area, my chances of hooking up increased dramatically when I could place the fly right where the fish were. Whether sight fishing the flats, casting to surface action, or placing your fly along the edges of mangroves, sod banks, or riplines, casting accuracy can and often will increase your odds of success.

SHOOTING LINE

Shooting line is a routine technique used by almost anybody who fly fishes in salt water. However, many folks fly fishing in fresh water do not shoot line, especially those fishing smaller trout rivers and streams. I observe this time and again when conducting casting classes or seminars in saltwater fly fishing. The concept of shooting line is foreign to many folks. If you are contemplating fly fishing in salt water and do not know how to shoot line or haven't used the technique frequently enough to be very comfortable with it, you will need to become proficient in it if you are to become more successful in saltwater fly fishing.

You can shoot line on either the forward or backcast or both. To shoot line, simply make a normal cast—except after you've made the short speedup and *stop* at the end of the cast, immediately release your grip on your line hand by making an "okay" sign with your fingers. Your thumb and forefinger will act like a circular rod guide, allowing the fly line to shoot between your fingers and out the rod tip. You can control how much line to shoot by closing down the "okay" sign and gently applying pressure to the fly line with your fingers. The amount of line you'll be able to shoot will depend on the amount of line (mass) that you have in the air, how much the rod is loaded/flexed as a result of this mass, the length of the casting stroke, and the line's velocity.

For example, if you were to make a forward cast with a short speedup and *stop* at the end of the cast to load the rod, and had 25 feet of fly line in the air on your last backcast, you could expect to shoot about an additional 10 to 15 feet (approximately 50 percent) of fly line on the final forward cast or a total distance of about 35 to 40 feet. Now, if you were to make an additional false cast and slip out a total of, say, 40 to 50 feet of fly line in the air on your second/last backcast, you might be able to shoot as much as 20 or 30 feet of fly line on your final forward cast or a total distance of about 60 to 80 feet. The second cast was made the same way, but you were able to shoot more line simply because the additional fly line or mass caused the rod to load (bend) more deeply, which in essence transferred more energy to carry the 20 to 30 feet of additional line to the target before slowing down. If a haul is added at the end of the final forward cast, even greater distances can be achieved.

Learning how to shoot line proficiently is one of those magical moments for fly casters. Having the ability to cast an additional 10, 20, or even 30 feet of line and more without excessive false casting enables anglers to quickly deliver the fly and reach areas otherwise unattainable.

DISTANCE

I think it may be fair to say that in most fishing situations encountered by most saltwater fly fishermen, casting distance is probably the most significant limiting factor. Yes, there are lots of situations where distance is not an important consideration, but by and large we have to cover a lot of water or get to waters that are otherwise out of reach. In the Tropics and semi-Tropics, anglers may have to keep away from the mangroves for fear of spooking wary fish. While fishing the flats, the boat may just run out of water, leaving it up to the angler to cover the remaining distance with a long cast back into some really skinny stuff to reach a bonefish or snook. Along shores and beaches, the occasional blitzes or structures that hold fish may only be accessible with a long cast. For many anglers fishing along shorelines, being able to cover a lot of water with the fly is paramount in catching fish. The longer the cast, the more water can be covered. With all other things equal, the angler who covers the most water usually wins.

I often fish from a boat in my home waters along the mid-Atlantic coast—the Delaware and Chesapeake Bays—for species such as striped bass, gray trout, bluefish, and false albacore. To find these fish, I seek out structures/areas that usually hold fish such as deep-water rips, jetties, bridges, submerged rock piles, edges of channels, inlets, and the like. While cruising from one area to the next, I'll be also looking for bird activity that may indicate surface-feeding fish. Once a fishy location is found, I'll try to confirm the presence of fish with a fish finder if possible. After that, it's a matter of setting up a drift and blind casting along the edges of the feeding school, current, or structure. In my experience, if two anglers are essentially using the same lines, flies, and retrieve, the angler who can cast the farthest will usually catch more and often bigger fish. This makes sense for two very good reasons: First, the angler casting longer distances will have his fly in the water longer since he makes fewer casts, and second, longer casts simply

ADJUSTING YOUR CASTING STROKE

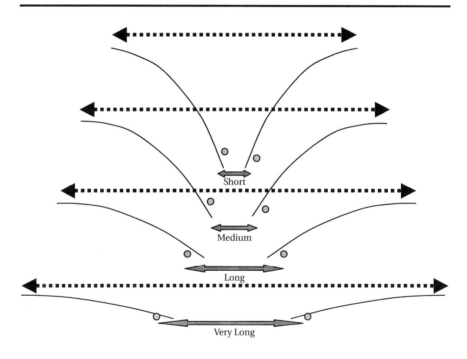

Become a more proficient caster by adjusting the length of your casting stroke to correspond to the distance and/or difficulty of the casts you need to make. Lengthen your casting stroke to cast longer distances, to make it easier to cast heavier flies or just to make it easier to cast all day long.

Notice the change in the position of the hand necessary to accomplish longer casting strokes.

cover more water, with the likelihood of being seen by more fish. Another benefit of being able to make longer casts is that larger fish will often take the fly at the maximum distance from the boat. Yes, I've had some big fish take the fly right next to the boat, but I can't tell you how many times I've made long casts of 70 feet or more and had a big fish take the fly on the first or second strip. My belief is that the bigger fish are much more wary and keep their distance from any suspicious noise from a boat or a wading angler, no matter how quiet you think you are.

To increase your casting distance, you need to move the rod through a longer casting stroke. The longer casting stroke will enable you to easily carry more line in the air and will give you more time to smoothly develop line speed before the speedup and *stop* at the end of the casting stroke. A basic rule of thumb is that the longer the casting stroke, the easier it is to cast, and the shorter and faster the speedup and *stop* at the very end of the casting stroke, the tighter the loop and the greater the distance you will achieve.

Now, in order to make that longer casting stroke, you need to shift your back foot so you are facing slightly sideways at a 45-degree angle. With your forearm also tilted outward at a 90-degree angle, you will be able to easily and smoothly pull your rod hand/rod tip all the way back along a low (almost) horizontal plane in a straight line 180 degrees from the target so that your arm and rod are nearly or completely extended at the end of the backcast. If you tried to make this cast facing forward, your body's own anatomy would prevent you from fully extending your rod hand back in a straight line. However, turning slightly sideways and moving your hand and rod tip along a low horizontal plane parallel to the surface of the water will enable you to fully extend on the backcast. This will enable you make a very long forward-casting stroke. You may need to shoot a little line out and make two backcasts in order to have approximately 50 to 60 feet of line in the air on your final backcast.

When the line on the final backcast looks like a horizontal candy cane, begin your forward cast slowly and smoothly. No power is needed, and there's no need to rush. As you gradually come forward, bring your rod hand closer to your body so the rod tip will begin tracking forward in a more vertical path. Smoothly and gradually increase the speed of your forward cast and finish with a very short, quick speedup and *stop* while aiming the rod tip upward toward the ten o'clock position and shooting the line.

By adding a double haul as described below, you can load the rod even more and cast farther by doing a short, quick (6- to 8-inch) haul at the same time as the short, quick speedup and *stop* at the very end of the cast. A long smooth casting stroke coupled with a very short, quick speedup and *stop* is key to distance casting.

Whether you're wading or fishing from a boat, using a stripping basket (see Strategy 7) can help maximize the distance of your casts. It will prove invaluable in keeping your line free from surface-tension effects of water when wading, from getting tangled up underfoot and getting washed ashore while fishing the surf, or getting tangled around something in the boat.

DOUBLE HAULING

Double hauling is just as important as shooting line. They are often used in conjunction with one another—first, to load the rod more, and second, to shoot line over greater distances without the need to false cast. The double haul is basically two single hauls done in the same casting series—one on the backcast and one on the forward cast. I frequently run into folks who fly fish fresh water and think double hauling is a casting technique used strictly for salt waters or only necessary when casting long distances. The fact of the matter is, the double haul makes any casting easier (fresh or salt), less tiresome, and, yes, it can add greater distances to your casts if needed. The greater line velocity that can be created also makes casting in windy conditions easier.

This past year I had an opportunity to do some fly fishing for silver salmon in Alaska's Chuit River on the north side of Cook Inlet opposite the Kenai Peninsula. Although the river was more a creek (only 30 or 40 feet across) after the spring runoff, the water was all the more clear and required longer casts to prevent alerting the salmon to my presence. Although it required casts of between 50 and 65 feet, I would routinely position myself on the now-exposed gravel bars along the river. I had a good vantage point for sight casting to the silvers while still keeping my distance. Using the double-haul technique, I could easily pull the entire fly line from the water with a haul on the backcast and make the final haul on the forward cast, setting the fly down upstream on a 45-degree angle along the opposite bank where the silvers were lying in the deeper water. Even though I was using a 3- to 3½-inch marabou streamer and a 5-foot sinking tip, the casting was effortless with the double haul. After seeing me land several silvers in short order, my guide—who was watching from a distance—came over and asked me why I was using a double haul when it really wasn't necessary (his opinion). I politely explained that it made the casting much easier. He raised his eyebrows and simply said, "Oh."

After setting up the other clients in the group downstream, the guide watched me pluck a few more silvers and a couple of humpies from the stream. He was soon standing nearby asking if I was doing okay and if I needed anything. He eventually spoke up and said, "I see you're still double hauling." I guess that was my cue, so I asked the guide if he double hauled at all when he fished. He told me no, so I asked if he'd like to learn. He mentioned that he always likes to learn something new and eagerly took the rod. Within about 15 minutes or so, my guide was getting the hang of it and was double hauling fairly well. He was quite surprised at how effortless it was to cast and realized one of the reasons why I was hooking up with more fish than others in the party: Fewer backcasts were required to cast the same distance. This meant that my fly was in the water and in front of fish for a longer amount of time and increased my hook-ups. He thanked me and said he'd better leave me alone so I could get back to fishing. I agreed.

Hauling (single or double) essentially involves using the nonrod or line-control hand to pull sharply down about 6 to 8 inches in one quick motion at the same time that the rod hand speeds up and *stops* at the end of each forward or backcast. This causes the rod to flex or load even more at the brief moment just before the cast is made. This additional energy is transferred to the the fly line, making any cast easier and making longer casts possible.

Lefty Kreh's technique for teaching the double haul is the best that I know. In his video *Lessons with Lefty,* he teaches the double haul in such a way that practically anyone can learn in just a few minutes. The secret of his technique is that he has his students break down and practice the double haul as two separate single hauls. First the student will do a single back haul on the pickup and let the fly line straighten out on the ground behind him. With the rod tip down, the student will then remove any slack and make a single forward haul—the second part of the double haul—letting the line straighten out on the ground. This process is repeated again and again until the student gets the feel of this somewhat awkward motion. Once he's comfortable making each separate back and forward haul with quicker timing, the student then attempts to link them together while keeping the fly line in the air. Usually a new student will only be able to make several double hauls before the cast falls apart, in which case he merely repeats the process until he eventually gets the rhythm and timing down.

A misconception is that a longer haul is needed for a longer cast. This is simply not true. It may look impressive, but it's not effective. For longer casts, use the same 6- to 8-inch haul, but increase the speed of the hauling motion. Lefty personally showed me how to do this one properly—and man, what a difference! In this case, quicker equals longer. Muscle has nothing to do with it. It's all technique.

BACKCASTING

Whether you refer to it as the Barnegat Cast, the Sianora Sling, or just plain ol' backcast, being able to deliver the fly on the backcast is very useful. Backcasting along the Jersey shore is quite effective combating the prevailing southwesterly winds, which have a tendency to blow the line and fly in the direction of the angler (right-hand casters). To overcome this, Jersey anglers fishing the suds simply turn their backs to the wind, face Barnegat Bay, and deliver the fly on the backcast. Since the mechanics of the forward and backcasts are the same, the technique is easily learned. I use the Barnegat Cast frequently along the Jersey shore while fishing for stripers when those darn southwesterly winds blow. More recently, Mark Sedotti used a similar approach with his Sianora Sling in making longer casts while backcasting. Backcasting serves both these purposes well. However, when I was fully entrenched in trout fishing, I can honestly say that I never routinely used or saw anyone else using backcasts to deliver the fly.

When saltwater fly fishing, you learn early that the more tricks you have in your bag, the better prepared you are if an unusual situation arises. Such was the case one late April while fishing the Jersey shore. The evening before I had fished Corson Inlet on an incoming tide and caught numerous 3- to 5-pound bluefish well into dark. Having spring fever, I decided to fish the inlet again the next evening. The conditions would be about the same, and the blues ought to be there. I arrived just before sundown and discovered that it was much windier than I expected. It was blowing a good 25 mph with higher gusts. As I made the long walk out to the southern side of the inlet, I had to walk backward to shield my face from the blowing sand. It was a nor'easter, and man was it blowing. I was ready to call it quits and go home when I spotted a single tiny figure in the deepening dusk at the edge of the sandbar. It looked like a surf caster. I figured that since I'd driven an hour to get here, I might as well give it a shot.

When I got to the high-tide mark I saw a 5-gallon bucket with a fly rod in it; there was the angler throwing metal to busting blues in the inlet just off the edge of the bar. I made my way out to the edge of the bar a short distance away from the other angler and could see that the blues this evening were a bit larger, in the 5- to 8-pound range. The blues were really having a hoot in the choppy inlet and were busting all over the place—unfortunately, not very close. I needed to make a long cast to reach them, but when I got into casting position, I found myself facing north with the wind blowing hard on my casting side. There was no way I was going to make a 30-foot cast, let alone 60 feet or more. Although a southwesterly wind was not blowing, I could still use the same basic concept as the Barnegat Cast. Pausing a moment, I switched my stance, placing my back toward the wind. I'm not saying it was easy, but after backcasting a few times, my line soon came tight with a nice 8-pound bluefish. I could just reach the edge of the feeding fish, and every few casts I would hook up. And I was thinking about going home!

As just described, backcasting can keep your line and fly away from your body, and it can often enable you to cast farther to reach an otherwise unobtainable target. Backcasting can provide some additional benefits as well. When fishing from shore, your casting possibilities are essentially 180 degrees, forward and to each side. However, when fishing from a boat, your casting possibilities double to a full 360 degrees. Wow! That's a lot more water to cover. If you have the mind-set that you should only cast on the forward cast, as most anglers do, then you are limiting yourself to that 180 degrees. I suggest increasing your angling opportunities 100 percent by being prepared to deliver the fly on either the forward or back cast.

On my first false albacore trip, I booked Capt. Sarah Gardner (Horsley) as my guide. Not only is Sarah one heck of a guide, but she is also an exceptional fly caster. She located scattered pods of breaking albies out on the ocean in front of the Cape Lookout Lighthouse. I took up position in the bow as Sarah skillfully positioned the boat so that I could make forward casts with my right hand, rod and fly over the bow where it was unobstructed and I didn't have to worry about hitting the center console. Two false casts later I was tight to an albie now heading quickly to Europe. We repeated this scenario several more times. After releasing the third fish and getting my rod in hand, Sarah pointed to a pod of albies off the starboard side about the four o'clock position and asked if I could reach them on my backcast. I said I would give it a try. Without moving my feet, I quickly let out a forward cast of about 40 feet or so and then shot my backcast the 60 feet to the fish. The fly landed softly in the middle of the commotion and was quickly engulfed by a busting albie. Yahoo! Many anglers can cast a country mile going forward. However, in order to be versatile, anglers need to be able to deliver a fly on the backcast with distance and accuracy.

If you are one of the lucky ones who own and operate a boat, you have probably found yourself setting up your fishing buddies according to their casting preference, not your own. I'm right-handed, as you already know. My problem is all of my fishing buddies are also right-handed. When you're right-handed and fishing in the bow, you can easily make casts off the port or left side of the boat from around the eight o'clock to eleven o'-clock positions. This would place your right rod hand and fly off the bow without any worry of hitting obstructions like the center console, vertically stored rods, and so on. Under most fishing scenarios when drifting, fishing around structure, or working a school of breaking fish, both anglers will need to fish off the same side of the boat, which for right-handed anglers is usually going to be the port side. This poses a slight problem for the person in the back of the boat if he is right-handed. He will need to either cast across his body to get his backcast and fly off the back of the boat or raise his arm to cast higher overhead to miss the center console. Either way makes for a tiresome day when making hundreds of blind casts, especially with weighted lines.

As a captain often faced with this situation, my solution is to deliver the fly on the backcast. To accomplish this, simply turn sideways facing the back of the boat, then make a forward cast as you normally would off the starboard or right side of the boat. This will place your rod and fly off the stern of the boat and out of harm's way. After your first or second forward cast (depending upon the target's distance), make a final backcast as you normally would and shoot the line, being sure to point the rod tip at the intended target. If you have not tried this, you'll be amazed at how easy and accurate the backcast is.

Whether fishing for bonefish, redfish, false albacore, or stripers, an angler who can deliver the fly accurately backcasting will be much better prepared and able to take advantage of what fishing opportunities present themselves. Sometimes there is only a thin sliver of an opportunity. Be prepared and you'll be more successful.

SPEED CASTING

When you think of the need to deliver the fly quickly to the target, visions of flats fishing for the big three—tarpon, bonefish, and permit—probably comes to mind. These species typically cruise the flats or their edges in search of prey and are generally always on the move. Being nearly invisible complicates matters more. There is often only a narrow window of opportunity in which to deliver the fly. On average, maybe it's only five or six seconds. That's it! Take too long to present the fly and the fish may have since changed direction or have disappeared from sight. The fly may be presented where the fish was rather then where it is, or the angler may line the fish, spooking it. In either case the opportunity is usually lost. Being quick at the draw is key to winning this game on a consistent basis.

My early experiences fly fishing for bonefish taught me well the importance of delivering the fly quickly, but they didn't teach me how. I learned

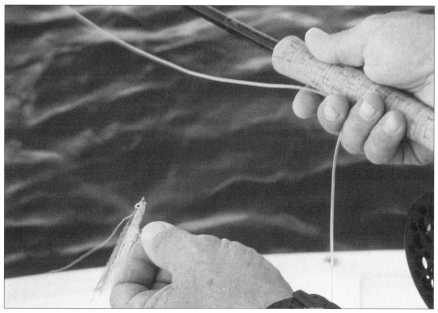

Sight fishing requires quick accurate casts. Here an angler is set and ready to make a speed cast when a fish is spotted.

how to cast quickly off the water before I actually went fishing. Thinking that you can learn anything when you're in sight of a bonefish and your heart is racing is just nonsense. It's not going to happen. The best time to learn is when you're not fishing, when you can give your full concentration to casting. The rest is fairly easy.

To make a cast quickly, you must be capable of loading the rod and developing sufficient line speed quickly. Most anglers try to do this unsuccessfully by starting out with only a minimum of line outside the rod tip, which will require a good number of false casts to eventually load the rod. Instead an angler should start with approximately 15 to 20 feet of fly line outside the rod tip. This amount of line will be sufficient to reach a target 20 to 25 feet away as is, and also has enough weight to sufficiently load the rod to cast double that distance (40 to 50 feet) with just one false cast or cast 60 to 80 feet with only two false casts. What do you do with all that line, you ask? The extra line is usually dragged in the water if you're wading the flats. If you're fishing from a boat, be sure to drag it in the water along the downcurrent side, being careful not to get it caught under the boat. I fish out of an 18-foot center console that has considerable freeboard. On certain occasions when fishing for stripers and albies, it is necessary to speed cast. What I typically do is strip 15 or 20 feet of fly line out of the rod tip and lay it on the deck of the cockpit, being sure not to step on it. I can't load the rod quite as quickly as when I'm in the water, where I can use the water's surface tension, but it works almost as well.

To practice the speed cast, find an open area like a large lawn, park, or ball field and shake 15 to 20 feet of line outside your rod tip, including your leader, being sure not to step on the line. Then pinch the fly or some yarn between your thumb and forefinger at the bend of the hook, being certain to keep the point of the hook outside and away from your hand. Since you won't be casting with water tension helping to load the rod, this will be essentially just like having the line stacked inside on the boat deck.

Look for a target 20 to 25 feet away and keep your eyes focused on it. This is essential since speed casting is used in conjunction with sight fishing. If you only practice the speed part, you'll never develop the accuracy part, thereby missing fishing opportunities when you get on the water. Then with your target in focus and slight tension on the fly/yarn, point the rod forward and make a firm backcast while still maintaining your grip on the fly/yarn. This will help load the rod. If you've made a good firm backcast with a short speedup and *stop,* the fly/yarn will be pulled from your fingers at that point. Now make a standard forward-casting stroke at the target. Hopefully, you'll either hit your target or come very close. If not, don't worry. Practice this short speed cast several more times and you'll find your rhythm and timing improving. Stop for a minute and think what you've just accomplished. You have just made a very accurate cast of 20 to 25 feet with only one backcast in about three seconds. To hit a different target at a different angle, just reposition your feet so you are facing your new target and repeat. Practice this short cast until you can deliver the fly to various targets at different angles with consistency and comfort.

It's important to remember that the "speed" of this cast comes not so much from a dramatic increase in the speed of the casting stroke as it does from minimizing the number of false casts you need to make to reach the target. In this first example, you cast only 20 to 25 feet. That is the same amount of line that you had outside your rod tip. All you did was get the line in motion on the backcast and then come ahead with a standard forward cast and easily make a 20-foot cast. If you had difficulty making the cast, shorten up and start with 10 or 15 feet. Keep in mind that you will learn casting faster by starting with a shorter line. Don't get too anxious about trying to cast a long line right away. Many anglers attempt this only to find that they have greater difficulty learning the technique. The macho muscle thing usually just causes mucho problems. Put your muscles and ego aside. Technique has very little to do with muscles and certainly nothing to do with ego.

Now you're ready to make an accurate speed cast to a target 50 to 60 feet away using just two backcasts. Start the cast using 20 feet of line outside your rod tip. The difference is, do a double haul on the first forward cast and shoot about 5 to 10 feet of line. This will now give you 25 to 30 feet of line already in the air. On the second backcast, which will be a full standard backcast, double haul and shoot an additional 5 to 10 feet of line out. You will now have between 30 and 40 feet of line in the air. On the final cast, do a short quick 6- to 8-inch haul to increase the bend or load of the rod and shoot the remaining line necessary (15 to 20 feet) to hit the target 45 to 60 feet away. With a little practice, you'll be able to speed cast comfortably to targets 60 feet away or more with just two backcasts. All of this accomplished in about 5 or 6 seconds.

As with any new technique, practice will make perfect. This is a great technique to practice since it combines all the mechanics of basic casting, plus accuracy, distance, double hauling, shooting line, and speed of delivery. The speed cast is an essential part of flats fishing, but it is also very effective when stripers and especially albies get a little spooky. After learning this technique, you'll be ready to deliver the fly quickly and accurately when an opportunity presents itself.

SINKING LINES/SHOOTING HEADS

Unfortunately, many wannabe saltwater fly rodders suffer from fear of casting sinking lines. This phobia prevents many anglers, especially those who fish deeper in the water column, from achieving more success. If there is one unjustified claim by anglers fly fishing the salt, it's that more heavily weighted sinking lines are difficult to cast. It was late December, and I was out striper fishing off the Jersey coast with my good friend Greg Mentzer. We didn't find any surface-feeding fish, but we found a nice pod down deep in about 20 feet of water off Seaside Park. Like any good striper fly fishermen should be off Jersey, we were prepared with a variety of sinking lines. There was a stiff breeze blowing out of the west, but with Teeny 550s (sink rate of 9 inches per second) we were in the strike zone and bailing stripers on a regular basis with each drift. There was another boat jigging the same area with conventional gear. Over the radio, the captain of the other boat gave us a call and asked what type of lines we were using and mentioned that he would really like to catch some of these stripers on the fly like we were doing. Greg picked up the receiver and gave a shout back and told him what we were using. There was a long pause before the other captain came back on the radio and said that he had similar sinking lines, but it was too windy to use them. He must have been just a little curious as to how we were casting with the same lines and went on to ask if we were having difficulty casting into the wind. I guess he was in disbelief when Greg told him we were having no difficulty; he never responded again on the radio. Sinking lines work exceptionally well in the wind. Greg and I just shrugged our shoulders and continued catching stripers until the tide quit.

Anyone who feels sinking lines are difficult to cast really does not understand how to cast with them. Sinking lines need to be cast differently than conventional fly lines. Unlike conventional lines, sinking lines have a very heavily weighted forward section (24 to 30 feet or more) as compared to the thinner/lighter running line to which it is seamlessly attached. This causes a slight hinging effect, which can create slack line and difficulty

One of the finest fly anglers I know is Carol Mentzer. In this photo Carol is casting a 550-grain weighted line to late-summer stripers in the middle Chesapeake. Note the steep angle and tremendous load of the rod, making long casts almost effortless.

when casting. The hinging effect is similar to a door moving freely back and forth—or in this case up and down—on its hinges. This effect is formed where the heavier weighted portion (more rigid) of the line joins the thinner running line (less rigid/more flexible). A hinging effect may be good for doors, but it's not good for casting. It can create waves and slack in the thinner/lighter running line that will need to be removed before making the cast. Shooting-head systems are similar, except the forward section is attached with a loop-to-loop connection to a thinner running line to facilitate removal and replacement with a different head (such as floating, intermediate, or sinking). Although a little rough on the hands and fingers, I prefer braided mono running lines since they are very slick and shoot well through the guides and tangle far less than other running lines.

Shooting-head systems, however, tend to have a greater hinging effect, making them a little more difficult to cast. With sinking lines or shooting heads, you do not want a short speedup and *stop* at the end of the casting stroke creating a tight loop. This overshocks the rod and can create all kinds of waves and slack in the line. Instead, you'll want almost the exact opposite. Sounds a bit odd after everything I've said so far, doesn't it? But this is where most anglers get confused when casting sinking lines/shooting heads. They try to use the same technique as with floating or intermediate fly lines, and it doesn't work. With sinking lines/shooting heads, you want to create more open casting loops to avoid these problems.

To begin with, sinking lines/shooting heads cannot be lifted from the surface like floating lines. First you must retrieve the running line until the sinking-tip section plus about 1 or 2 feet of the running line is outside the rod tip. Make one or two roll casts if needed to get the sinking portion of the line to the surface and *immediately* begin a low backcast to prevent the line from sinking. This is very important—if you hesitate even a little, the sinking portion of the line will have started to sink, making it very difficult to lift the line from the water on the backcast. Make your backcast low with your rod moving almost parallel to the water (see "Casting Sinking Lines/Shooting Heads," page 49). Keep your rod tip moving the entire time as you scribe a curved or elliptical path with one continuous movement on the backcast rather than the speedup and *stop.* As you come around the elliptical path, begin the forward cast by accelerating and loading the rod fully down to the butt section with a nice smooth casting stroke. Now all you have to do is make a forward cast as you would normally, but with a little wider loop, aiming it at an upward angle and forming an okay sign with your line hand. The line should shoot a considerable distance. If you haul the line at the end of the forward cast, the cast will be easier and will travel even farther.

I usually teach folks this cast by first starting with a sinking line of no more than 325 or 350 grains and only about 15 feet or so outside the rod tip. I then have them maintain their hold on the line as I have them move the line around and around in an elliptical path, but without actually casting. What this does is give you a good sense or feel of the rod loading and unloading. Once you're comfortable making those elliptical paths, you can

CASTING SINKING LINES/SHOOTING HEADS

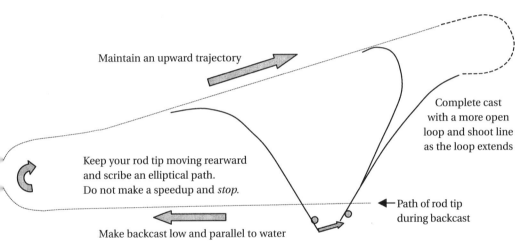

Maintain an upward trajectory

Complete cast with a more open loop and shoot line as the loop extends

Keep your rod tip moving rearward and scribe an elliptical path.
Do not make a speedup and *stop*.

Path of rod tip during backcast

Make backcast low and parallel to water

Sinking lines/shooting heads cannot be lifted from the surface like floating lines. First you must retrieve the running line until the weighted forward section plus about 1 to 2 feet of the running line is outside the rod tip. Make one or two roll casts if needed to get the weighted portion of the line to the surface and immediately begin a low backcast to prevent the line from sinking. Then complete the cast as described above. For longer shooting heads or if you are having trouble picking up the weighted portion of the line with the roll cast, strip in more line until you are able to comfortably pick up the line after a roll cast. You can make a cast with a portion of the weighted line inside the tip but it is more effective if you make a false cast and slip the weighted portion outside the tip first before making your final forward cast.

shoot the line at the end of the forward cast. Even if you have only 15 feet or so outside the rod tip, you should still be able to easily cast 50 to 60 feet with just one backcast. Always remember, these are weighted lines. If you don't aim up at about the ten-thirty position on your final cast, the line will quickly crash to the ground or water and will not go very far. Once you're comfortable with this amount of line, keep on extending more line outside the rod tip until you get the full weighted portion outside the tip plus about 1 or 2 feet of running line or until you've reached your comfort zone.

For those of you who have been casting sinking lines/shooting heads and have been double hauling for a while and want to get even more distance, try this. Start off with the sinking portion of the line and about 2 feet of running line outside the rod tip. Make your roll cast(s) to bring the line to the surface, then start your backcast by bringing your rod back in a slight upward motion almost parallel to the water, and do a haul to shoot an additional 5 to 10 feet of line. The important thing is, after you make the haul, drift or follow your rod tip back with the line to minimize any slack from forming. Your arm may need to be almost fully extended on your backcast before you begin to come forward nice and smoothly. This will minimize slack and eliminate the problems associated with the abrupt *stop* at the end of the backcast. It will also give you a maximum casting stroke and load on the forward cast. On your forward cast, your rod hand should move from approximately waist height to shoulder height or even a little higher. Finish the forward cast with a final haul and by stabbing the rod tip forward to between the ten and eleven o'clock positions. This upward trajectory will allow the more heavily weighted sinking line/shooting head sufficient time to reach its target. With a little practice you should be able to easily cast the entire line and possibly more.

To make casting sinking lines/shooting heads even easier from a boat, use the backcast in conjunction with a water haul. A water haul uses the surface tension of the water to load the rod. It's achieved by simply casting, letting the fly line come in contact with the water, and then immediately making a forward or backcast. This creates a deep load in the rod that translates to more energy for easier casting and greater distances. If, for example, I was playing captain and had just set up a drift where we would be fishing off the port or left side of the boat, I would start by facing the back of the boat. First I would make a roll cast or two to get the sinking portion of the line to the surface off the left side of the boat. Then I would immediately turn my hips slightly and make a forward cast off the starboard or right side of the boat with a haul shooting an extra 10 to 15 feet of running line. As soon as the line touched the water, I would pivot my hips the other way and do a water haul on my backcast and finish the cast making a stabbing motion with the rod tip in a slight upward motion. The backcast coupled with the water haul and a bit of extra line will make it surprisingly easy to make exceptionally long casts all day long without fatigue. This is why, although I'm right-handed, I usually don't complain when I have to fish from the back of the boat using weighted lines. Backcasting with a water haul is a piece of cake. Give it a try. I'm sure you'll be pleasantly surprised.

Here are some suggestions to help improve your casting accuracy and distance:

- Practice your casting accuracy in a yard, park, or field and make it fun (not while fishing).
- Use half a dozen hula hoops, circles of heavy rope, or paper plates with large spikes to hold them in place for targets and position them at different distances and angles.
- Use a leader of only 4 to 6 feet, which will cover most saltwater situations, and tie on a small piece of yarn about the size of the end of your pinkie.
- Start with short distances of 20 to 40 feet first. Then increase to 40 to 60 feet, 60 to 80 feet, and more if you can make the distance. Timing is everything. Make smooth, controlled casting strokes.
- Use double hauling in combination with shooting line at the end of the cast to improve effectiveness.
- First try using a maximum of three false casts to reach these targets. Once you're able to consistently do that, reduce your false casting to a maximum of only two.
- Once you're comfortable working these distances separately, try mixing up your targets at a wide variety of distances and angles. Remember to keep your false casting to a minimum and point the rod tip toward the target.
- Next, try speed casting to the same targets.
- After you've practiced forward casts, do the same exercises backcasting.
- Then practice forward and backcasting to the targets using different weighted lines.

STRATEGY 2—BECOME A PROFICIENT CASTER

Casting proficiently is the most important difference between catching fish and not catching fish in salt water. To be more successful, develop the ability to . . .

- Apply good casting mechanics.
- Cast accurately.
- Shoot line.
- Cast greater distances.
- Double haul.
- Deliver the fly on the backcast.
- Speed cast.
- Cast sinking lines/shooting heads effectively and efficiently.

SPEND TIME ON THE WATER

You can do all the reading in the world. You can be the best caster and have the best flies, but if you don't spend time on the water, you'll never realize your fullest potential, since you won't know enough about the where, when, and how of fishing salt waters. You see, there's no substitute for time spent on the water. Even though I spend a considerable amount of time on the water, I'm still learning every time I'm out there. Now, don't misunderstand me. I'm not suggesting that you need to spend as much time on the water as I do before you improve your success. What I am suggesting is that if you were to spend more time than you are now on the water and apply what I am suggesting in this chapter, you will be more successful over time. I'll say it again . . . there's no substitute for time spent on the water. How much time you'll need to spend will depend to a large extent on your ability to observe and learn, the size and nature of the waters you're trying to learn, and your desire to be more successful as a saltwater fly fisher. As the saying goes, *Anything worth having is worth working for.*

Besides fishing, you need to spend time on the water to learn more intimate knowledge and skills about three important things:

1. Where to fish.   2. How to spot fish.   3. When to fish.

But first, you need to understand how to observe and learn.

OBSERVE AND LEARN

Anglers who are willing to make a conscientious effort to observe and actively learn the significance of what they are seeing will be more successful over time. This is especially true when on the water. Some observations can be very obvious, while others are quite subtle.

Here's a situation that we can use as an example to help illustrate what I'm talking about:

You're cruising in your ATV or boat along an unfamiliar stretch of water in search of a likely place to catch striped bass and notice a large number of birds hovering over the water some distance away. As you approach, you observe that the birds are working very close to the surface and are occasionally dipping into the water. You also observe that there is a noticeable current in the area of otherwise calm water. Upon closer examination, you notice boils and dorsal and tail fins just breaking the surface slightly every once in a while along the edges of the current.

Okay, let's list some of the **obvious observations** and their significance:

Hovering birds in the distance. Could mean that bait and predatory fish (stripers) are in the area.

Birds working close to the water and diving. Predatory fish are probably working bait near the surface making it easier to attack.

Current in the area. Predatory fish are attracted to currents since they carry and disorient bait, making it easy prey.

Boils from predatory fish and some evidence of dorsal and tail fins. Predatory fish are present at and near the surface. A floating or intermediate line may be best.

Birds sitting on the water. Bait and predatory fish could be underneath.

Any angler would be fortunate to run into this situation. There's a good chance you'll catch some fish this time, but what about next time? I don't know about you, but I always want to increase my odds of success each time I go back on the water. The more I can observe and learn, the better the likelihood that I can predict where and when I stand a very good chance of catching fish.

Now let's take the same example as above and try to identify other more subtle things we can learn from posing some questions to ourselves when we're in one of these situations.

What types of birds are they? Small birds like terns usually means smaller bait (rainbait, bay anchovies, silversides, and the like). This would greatly help in selecting the right size and profile of fly.

Heavy concentration of birds working over surface-feeding stripers in the middle Chesapeake. (Photo: Greg and Carol Mentzer)

Do the birds occasionally have a bait dangling from their mouth? If so, how big is it, and what does it look like? Sometimes you can actually see and estimate the size of the bait the birds and predatory fish are feeding on. Again, this would greatly help in selecting the right size, profile, and perhaps color of fly.

Are the predatory fish showing themselves with violent surface splashes and jumps, or are they just boiling or finning the surface, or are they completely below the surface? In this example, the fish are mostly boiling at or near the surface, indicating that it would probably be best to use an intermediate line to get the fly down a little into the strike zone. Sometimes this, along with the presence of mostly terns, can indicate that the bait may be quite small, like rainbait, bay anchovies, or possibly silversides. You would be better able to select the right fly.

What is your exact location via a GPS? If you don't have one, are there any visible landmarks on shore? Your exact location may not be important to know now, but it will be if you want to ever find the same spot again.

What is the tide stage? Is it the beginning, middle, or end of the outgoing or incoming tide? Knowing the correct tide stage is critical for many species, especially stripers. Tidal movement creates currents that carry bait and attract predatory fish. However, depending upon where you are, sometimes one tide or part of the tide is better than another.

What is the moon phase? Full- and new-moon phases cause higher- and lower-than-normal tidal stages. Movements of baitfish from back bays and spawning are typically aligned with these same phases.

What time of day is it—A.M. OR P.M.? Time of day can be very important depending upon the species of fish you're after. Stripers predominantly feed at night or during low-light conditions. Bonefish may only be on the flats early in the morning while the water is cooler and leave when the sun heats the water above their comfort level.

What day of the week is it? Some of the more productive fish locations may have excess boat traffic. Many species such as sea trout, stripers, and bonefish do not like the noise and will usually leave the area or stop feeding. Weekdays may be the only time the location is quiet and productive for fishing from either a boat or shore.

What's the date? Time of year is very important. A few weeks, let alone months, can make a huge difference. Many fish along the Atlantic coast like striped bass, specks, and redfish migrate and, as such, just may not be in a particular location with any certainty until a certain time of year. This also applies to baitfish.

What are the weather conditions? Cold fronts, overcast days, rainy days, sunny days—all affect the quality of fishing to some degree. For some species, weather may be more important than others. While overcast days are generally great for stripers, they're terrible for bonefish and redfish because of the lack of visibility when sight fishing. Wind can also be an important factor. There's usually good fishing after and even during a nor'easter along the New England coast.

What is the water depth and contour of the bottom structure that created the current? The rip current in our example was probably caused by a bottom structure or feature. Rips are magnets for bait and predatory fish alike. Check the depth and contours of the bottom with a depth finder or by referring to the charts of the area.

What's the water temperature? All fish have a preferred temperature range. The ideal temperature for striped bass, for example, is about 55 degrees, plus or minus 10 degrees.

Did any fish that were caught spit up any bait and if so, what was it? What size, shape, and color? Many gamefish will spit up bait in and around the boat when caught. This is a great way to learn exactly what bait they're feeding on so you can match it.

Hopefully, this example has illustrated how important it is to make active observations while on the water. By being an active observer in this case, you would have learned over 200 percent more information than being just a casual observer. As you'll learn in strategy 7, the information you learn while spending time on the water will prove invaluable in planning successful fishing trips.

To ensure that you'll remember this information for the future, I highly recommend keeping a fishing diary. Records in your diary can be as detailed as you like, but my experience is that if you keep each entry short and include only the critical info as just reviewed, you'll probably be more likely to keep maintaining your diary. But if you spend too much time recording your entries, it becomes too much of a chore, and you'll probably stop doing it. So keep it short and simple. You'll be amazed at how fast you'll learn.

WHERE TO FISH

Many inshore game species prefer areas that have current or structure. Locations with both current and structure are ideal, since they often provide generous amounts of food. *Current* in this case refers to portions of water that are moving faster than the surrounding body of water. Many types of currents in fresh and salt water behave quite similarly. However, current in marine environments is created by tidal changes and strengthened by structures or features that constrict flow. Whereas in freshwater rivers and streams there is a relatively constant and continuous flow, in salt water there are six different periods of tide or current that occur daily—two incoming tides and two outgoing, with periods of slack water in between each. These tidal changes are caused primarily by the gravitational pull of the moon. During the new- and full-moon stages, the sun is aligned

Note the well-defined ripline formed by a sudden rise in the bottom at Cedar Point Rip, middle Chesapeake. Strong currents concentrate bait and are magnets for predatory fish. (Photo: Greg and Carol Mentzer)

in such a way as to cause extra-high and -low tides. Understanding tidal flows for the areas you are fishing is critical to your angling success. This goes for bone- or redfishing on the flats as well as for striper fishing in New England. Fluxes between low and high tides can vary widely depending upon your latitude. Having an intimate understanding of tidal conditions is also critically important to your personal safety when shore or wade fishing.

Predatory fish are attracted to areas of current for two primary reasons: Currents typically carry a wide array of bait including crabs, shrimp, and a wide assortment of baitfish; also, the fast-moving water tends to disorient bait, making it easy prey. Where there is current, there is usually a higher concentration of bait, simply because the higher volume of water that passes by a given area will be usually carrying a high volume of food with it. The faster the current, the more food is potentially available. What is also important to remember is that many species of marine life intention-

A RIP'S BOTTOM FEATURES AND TYPICAL HOLDING PATTERN

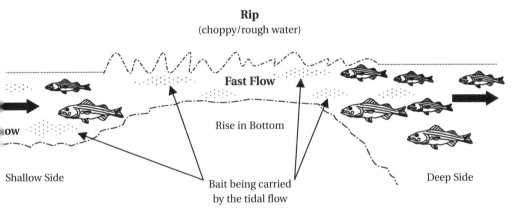

Rip
(choppy/rough water)

Fast Flow

Rise in Bottom

ow

Shallow Side

Bait being carried
by the tidal flow

Deep Side

Fish will typically station themselves above and below rips to take advantage of bait being concentrated and washed over shallow bars, reefs, or ledges. Each rip will be slightly different, depending upon the bottom features. Where fish station themselves may therefore vary slightly from rip to rip and from outgoing to incoming tides. Work the upcurrent side and the deeper holes where bait-and gamefish can accumulate on both the upcurrent and downcurrent sides.

ally station themselves in these locations because the currents will bring
the food to them. They don't have to waste energy finding the food.

To get a better idea of the benefits of current to fish, picture a large ex-
panse of water that has hundreds of baitfish, but they are scattered and
spread about an area of 4 square miles. If there were no current and you
were a predatory fish like a striper and wanted to eat, you would need to

**Fly rodders working the inside riprap shoreline, current edge, and points of Indian
River Inlet, Delaware at sunrise.**

exert energy in swimming around the area to first locate the scattered bait-fish, then to chase them down to eat them. This method of feeding isn't very energy-efficient for many inshore predatory fish. Now picture instead a nice cozy location alongside a ripline formed along a point of land or a bridge support where you could have some cover and be shielded from the tiring effects of the current. Here, you could sit in wait as the tidal currents flushed large quantities of food past you, and you could just dart out and snatch it up at your leisure. This is almost like sitting in a La-Z-Boy recliner and having a buffet of goodies moving by right under your nose. Needless to say, you would be very well fed.

Most inshore game species will seek out locations where rips form and set up shop. Of course, their presence will coincide with their migratory habits, preferred habitat, and (especially) tidal flow. To be routinely successful fly fishing for most saltwater species, you will also need to learn where these areas of rip currents are located. Incidentally, rips are formed by a variety of structures or bottom features that constrict the tidal flow. Navigational charts obtained from local bait shops and marinas provide a

FISHING ALONG A RIP

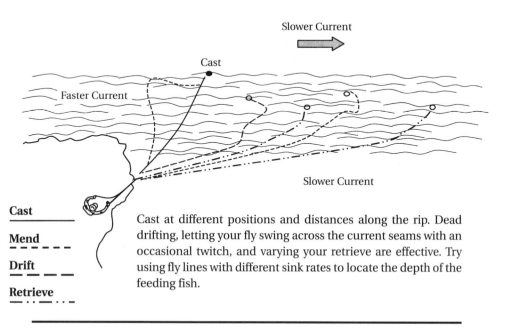

Slower Current

Cast

Faster Current

Slower Current

Cast

Mend

Drift

Retrieve

Cast at different positions and distances along the rip. Dead drifting, letting your fly swing across the current seams with an occasional twitch, and varying your retrieve are effective. Try using fly lines with different sink rates to locate the depth of the feeding fish.

wealth of information concerning structure, bottom features, and so on. As the tidal flow becomes constricted, the current increases. If you were to observe a common structure like a point of land or jetty during a flowing tide, there would be a noticeable rip formed on the downstream side. The tidal flow in this case is partially blocked. The water is being forced to constrict or become narrower, thereby increasing the current. Bottom features like submerged bars that rise from the bottom also form rips by forcing tidal flows to constrict. However, in this case the tidal flow of water is flattened vertically, thereby increasing flow. Just put your finger over the opening of a running garden hose and you'll get the picture.

Structures and bottom features that generate rips of varying intensities and will likely have fish at certain times include the following:

- Points of land or rock jutting out into open water (including island edges).
- Cuts, creek channels, and outlets in estuaries.
- Edges of oyster and sandbars.
- Open-water rip currents.
- Cuts in sandbars.
- Exposed and submerged rock piles.
- Wrecks large and small.
- Bridges, lighthouses, piers, pilings, and docks.
- Power-plant outflows and drainage ditches.

Rips can be recognized by the visible structures identified above and also by looking for the following:

- Noticeably faster flow than surrounding water.
- Areas or lines of darker water.
- Areas or lines of slightly disturbed or rough water.
- Foam and floating debris lines.
- Differences in clarity or water turbidity.

Note: Most rips are only noticeable when the tide is moving; some only at low tide.

Bottom or shoreline structures and features are also magnets for predatory fish since they attract bait and provide readily available food to predatory fish. These structures and features can take many forms and can vary from the complex—like a rocky shoreline—to a sand or mudflat, a bowl formed by a jetty along a beach, and something as small as a 2- by 6-foot depression in the bottom at the edge of a sandy beach. No matter how small a structure or feature may appear, never underestimate its ability to attract bait and predatory fish. Perhaps the best example of this that I can share with you occurred a number of years ago when I was fishing along the beaches of Marco Island in southwest Florida. It was early afternoon in July, and I was walking the beach sight fishing for snook. The tide was just starting to come in. The wind was light so the water clarity was quite good. I was hooking up with some nice 8- to 10-pound snook cruising 40 to 60 feet off the beach.

Because of this, I was focusing all my attention out away from the beach. As I walked along on the sand, there was a sudden commotion right by my feet. Looking down, I saw a nice snook bust out of a small 2-foot by 6-foot by 1-foot depression that was just inches from dry land. I was

FISHING THE MANGROVE EDGE

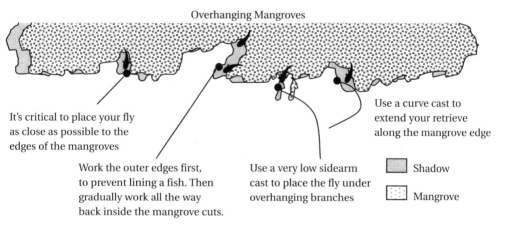

Overhanging Mangroves

It's critical to place your fly as close as possible to the edges of the mangroves

Use a curve cast to extend your retrieve along the mangrove edge

Work the outer edges first, to prevent lining a fish. Then gradually work all the way back inside the mangrove cuts.

Use a very low sidearm cast to place the fly under overhanging branches

Shadow

Mangrove

Fishing the mangrove edge for snook, redfish, baby tarpon, mangrove snapper, etc., poses its unique casting challenges and magical moments. Fish seek out the abundant variety of bait that call the underwater mangrove jungle home. During early morning and late afternoon, fish will station themselves in the shadowy edges to ambush their prey. As the sun rises and shadows diminish, the fish will drop back farther under the overhanging branches. Success will often be directly proportional to your ability to cast your fly within inches of the mangroves. Hang-ups will occur, but remember . . . if you're not hanging, you're not fishing.

amazed that a fish of that size would be so close to shore in broad daylight, with bathers walking up and down the beach.

Stepping back from the edge of the water to watch more closely, I noticed the gentle waves lapping up on the beach and could see small baitfish through the surface foam being washed into the small depression. It was just packed with bait. No wonder the snook was in there. Within a few minutes I noticed a long dark shadow ease back into the depression . . . it was the same snook returning to feed. I crouched down and got into a kneeling position about 15 feet off the water's edge and made a very short, soft cast just to the outside of the depression, then swam the fly into the hole. A few tiny strips later I was hooked up to a 10-pound snook. Incredible! It just goes to show that no structure or feature should ever be overlooked.

Some bottom and shoreline structures and features to target include the following:
- Sloughs, holes, or depressions that may develop along beaches or in estuaries.
- Shoreline bowls that can collect bait, especially when driven by the wind.
- Submerged rock piles and wrecks.
- Sand and mudflats that are rich in food (often high-tide-dependent).
- Mussel or oyster beds that are rich in food (often high-tide-dependent).

These bottom and shoreline structures and features can be recognized by:
- Observing the area at dead-low tide. Many will be readily visible at this time.
- Deeper water such as holes and sloughs may appear darker in color than surrounding water.
- Mussel and oyster beds may also appear darker in color than surrounding water, but indicate shallower water, so be cautious when approaching by boat.
- Using a depthfinder to mark the bottom contours.

Note: Use a fixed or portable GPS unit to mark productive structures and features.

Many areas of coastal waters also play host to large concentrations of fish due to migratory routes and the availability of bait. During these times of abundance, fish will be found in and around areas of current and structure, but will also be commonly found in open waters in pursuit of

A spring striper taken along the edge of a sandbar in Barnagat Bay, New Jersey. Note the dramatic change in color where the water is deeper. Predatory fish will cruise these edges, looking for bait to wash over the edge of the bar. To fish these edges effectively, be sure to stand back 30-40 feet from the edge to prevent spooking any fish.

schooled bait. Find the bait and you'll have a good chance of finding the fish. Here are just a few examples:

- The North Carolina coast, especially near Oregon Inlet, plays host to large schools of very large striped bass that winter over along the coast.
- The lower Chesapeake Bay, especially in and around the Chesapeake Bay Bridge Tunnel (CBBT), sees large schools of chopper blues in early to midspring.
- Delaware Bay and the Jersey coastal inlets and estuaries are invaded with tiderunner weakfish (gray/sea trout) in late April to late June.
- Cape Cod beaches during early fall for big striped bass.
- Montauk Point, New York, plays host to striped bass, blues, and false albacore from late summer into fall.
- The New York Bight area between Sandy Hook, New Jersey, and New York City is hot with false albacore, weakfish, bluefish, and striped bass from late summer into late fall.
- The Cape Lookout area of North Carolina becomes the epicenter for world-class false albacore fishing in early October to late November.
- The CBBT lights up with huge schools of medium to very large striped bass from late November into January.
- Boca Grande Pass in southwest Florida is the Super Bowl of fly fishing in spring, when large schools of giant tarpon take over the area.

HOW TO SPOT FISH

While it's important to know how to identify locations of current and structure while on the water, it's also wise to take advantage of some shortcuts if they present themselves to you. There are some obvious and subtle signs for spotting fish. To increase your odds of success in locating fish, you must learn to be observant and understand what you are seeing. Tools to help you see better include high-quality polarized sunglasses. I prefer medium to light amber-colored lens. These glasses greatly reduce glare and improve contrast, enabling you to see below the surface of the water. No angler should be without them. Additionally, make sure you have a pair of binoculars to enable you to see greater distances and to see some up-close detail of what's going on without having to move your position.

Large surface blitzes of feeding fish like stripers, bluefish, and false albacore, whether on the open water or along beaches, are without question the most obvious sign indicating the presence of fish. The glistening sprays of water and huge numbers of birds usually hovering over the action can often be seen with the naked eye several miles away. These large surfaces blitzes indicate huge numbers of fish. They can be as small as half an acre or as large as several square miles. Watching 20-pound-plus stripers crashing and leaping clear of the surface while chasing bait a foot or more in length is a sight to behold. With birds screeching, water splashing, and fish slurping down bait . . . it's incredible! These are truly magical moments. During some of these larger blitzes, not all the fish are on the surface at the same time. There may be scattered blitzes spread over several miles of open water or along stretches of beach. Under cloudy, rainy, or light foggy conditions, binoculars will be indispensable in locating these blitzes. There may also be large numbers of fish hidden below surface in, around, and between these blitzes. Monitor your fish finder to locate these fish. While you may find casting into the craziness at the surface irresistible, larger fish are often lurking well below the surface lazily feeding on the scraps sinking to the bottom. A sinking line, a large fly, and a slow retrieve could be your ticket to a big fish.

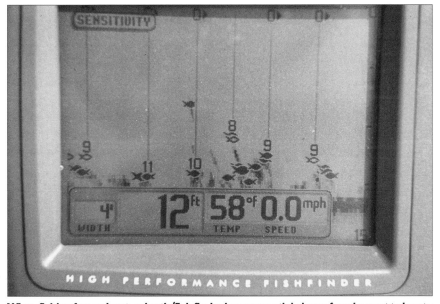

When fishing from a boat, a depth/fish finder is an essential piece of equipment to locate bottom structure and holding fish. In this situation, schooling fish were holding along the bottom in 8 to 12 feet of water. Weighted lines in the 450 to 550 range carried our flies quickly to our quarry.

Smaller surface blitzes are tougher to spot and often are much shorter in duration, causing them to be missed. Don't underestimate these smaller blitzes. Always keep alert and keep looking for positive signs of fish. Even just a few birds that continuously or periodically keep working the same area may be onto subsurface action or at least the presence of bait. Remember, find the bait, and eventually you'll find the predatory fish. When there is a rough chop on the water, fish usually become active. However, small surface blitzes may be camouflaged or sometimes just blend in with all the other white peaks. Learn to be even more observant in these situations. If you scan the water more closely, you may be able to spot an occasional fish breaking or clearing the water. Sprays of bait shooting above the surface like bright silvery shards of aluminum and an occasional bird or two may also give them away. Several years ago I was fishing with a few other friends in North Carolina for false albacore. My partner Rick Bender and I had a terrific day casting to small pods of blitzing albies in a heavy, tight chop. Back at the dock and over dinner, we learned that some friends who were fishing in another boat unfortunately never noticed the busting albies with all the heavy chop and missed out on all the action even though they fished the same areas during the same times.

Visible surface signs of fish include the typical "bust" or strike by a predatory fish like a snook, tarpon, striper, or even a redfish on or near the surface. This is a sure sign that fish are present, and they're what we call "Happy Fish"—fish that are relaxed, not alarmed, and eagerly feeding. These signs can, however, be camouflaged by whitecaps. To spot breaking fish in these tougher conditions, you have to look for more subtle and out-of-the-ordinary indications. A few other signs to look out for are surface boils and tailing or finning fish. Other more subtle signs of possible predatory fish include V wakes or "pushes" of water and "nervous water." As the name implies, there is a push of water caused by the fish's body displacing water as it moves in shallow water. This push forms a V shape or wake on the surface just *behind* the fish. When casting, remember to lead the fish by placing your fly several feet ahead of the wake. These signs are more easily seen in tannin-stained waters with dark bottoms like those of southwest Florida in the Ten Thousand Island area and all along the Gulf Coast and can often be seen from distances of 100 yards or more. They're less obvious to untrained eyes on the clear waters and lighter bottoms of many flats found in the Florida Keys, Bahamas, Caribbean, and Mexico, for example.

Nervous water can often indicate predatory fish, but often it's associated with a high concentration of bait at the surface. Sometimes predatory fish show up in short order, but unfortunately sometimes they don't . . . at least not when you or I are there. If there are no obvious signs of predation, watch the behavior of the school of bait for a while and see if portions of the bait along the outside fringes suddenly flash or move erratically. Sudden movements of the bait could indicate that there are a few predatory fish hanging around and charging the edges of the schools from time to time.

You must remember that you will probably not be alone in your quest of fish. When out on the water, whether you're fishing from a boat or the shore, it will help you to keep note of three other important indicators of potential fish—birds, people, and boats.

Birds working an area of surf, mangrove shoreline, or open water for any length of time is a good indication that bait is available and is probably worth checking out. There's no guarantee, but sooner or later predatory fish are bound to show up. Spotting people or boats along a certain stretch of beach or water may also indicate some possible action. If you're fishing from shore, don't limit yourself to just watching out for other surf fishermen. Also be sure to observe boats that are perhaps fishing just outside the breakers. If they are into fish, it could be just a matter of time before these fish are feeding in the surf. The opposite is true for you boaters. If you're running your boat along the beach, keep a watchful eye on the surf fishermen. If you spot some, see if they're hooking up. Often surf fishermen use four-wheel-drive vehicles on the beach. If you suddenly spot a number of vehicles zooming off in the same direction, it's a good bet they got a tip over the radio about some hot action. If you do observe some other anglers who are into fish, please be courteous and give them plenty of room to continue their fishing. If approaching by boat, be sure to idle down and approach quietly since you don't want to alarm the fish . . . or the anglers, for that matter. Stay a good distance outside their casting range.

WHEN TO FISH

By spending time on the water, you'll acquire a firsthand understanding of both seasonal migratory and daily feeding patterns of saltwater gamefish so that you'll be able to improve your odds of success by knowing better when to fish. Unlike most freshwater species, which usually spend their entire lives within a relatively small general area, saltwater gamefish seem to be almost always on the move and can travel hundreds of miles each year on their migratory routes. An area could switch from having almost no fish one week to having seemingly unlimited fish the next. For instance, the weather during the early fall of 2000 was quite mild in New England, which held the stripers at Montauk longer than anticipated. The ocean area just off Sandy Hook the first weekend of November was almost devoid of stripers, while just four days later in the exact same area when the fish pushed southward we found 10 square miles of fish from just off the beaches to 2 miles out. Wow . . . what a difference a few days can make! Even on a daily basis, certain areas might be totally devoid of gamefish in the morning and inundated with them that same afternoon. If you spend enough time on the water, you'll learn their ways and get your share of incredible action.

Rick Bender holds up a nice early-spring weakfish or gray sea trout taken from Barnegat Bay. Warm-water outflows of power-generation stations are usually the first and last holding locations for many migratory species.

There are a number of factors you need to consider in determining when to fish for certain species:

- ►◄ Water temperature.
- ►◄ Tidal stage.
- ►◄ Light.
- ►◄ Water clarity.
- ►◄ Wind.
- ►◄ Boat traffic.
- ►◄ Availability of bait.

Water Temperature

Water temperature is strongly influenced by the time of year or season. This is more important for those folks living farther north, where there are large seasonal differences of water temperatures, than for those living in more temperate climates in the southern Atlantic and Gulf states. In the more northern climates along the mid- and northern Atlantic coasts, the large climatic swings cause water temperatures to rise and fall dramatically, which triggers seasonal migrations of a number of sought-after gamefish, including redfish, bluefish, striped bass, and gray and speckled trout. Essentially, there is a spring migration beginning first in the more southern areas in early to mid-March as the coastal waters warm and gradually progressing northward well into May. Depending upon the particular temperature preferences, different species have different ranges that they will seek out for the remainder of the summer months before beginning their reverse migration route in the fall starting around October and extending well into December and beyond.

While there may be close approximations of when different species can be expected to pass through on their spring and fall migration routes, the exact timing of when this takes place will vary from year to year depending upon the weather conditions. It's important for you to spend time on the water to learn firsthand when different species are passing through on their migrations and which ones will be available in your fishing locations during the summer months. Besides learning when this actually takes place, you will also be exposed to some phenomenal fishing opportunities. Migrating fish usually travel in large numbers and are very aggressive while actively feeding. If you don't spend enough time on the water, you'll possibly miss out on the action. Be sure to review the examples of seasonal migrations included earlier in this chapter.

Tidal Stages

Learning when to fish during certain tidal stages will be a key factor to successful fly fishing in the salt. In general, most saltwater fish go off their feeding when the water goes slack between tide changes. It's like flipping the feeding switch off. You need to know this so you don't incorrectly schedule the start of your fishing during a slack tide or leave a productive area because the fish stopped biting. You must realize that the fish are just taking a short break. Many folks new to saltwater fishing, however, think it's time to move on and find a new location. I can't tell you how many times I've watched folks continue to fish hard through most of the slack tide and then leave out of frustration just minutes before the fishing heats right back up. Although it will vary from location to location, the most productive fishing takes place from about an hour after the tide begins to run to about an hour before it slackens. This is when the tidal flow is running hard and is pushing a lot of bait. Peak tidal flows vary from location to location, however.

The author casting to breaking fish at Thomas Point Light in the middle Chesapeake. While lighthouses and other structures may hold fish, most species will not actively feed unless the tide is running.

Tidal influences involving flats can be dramatic. At low tide many of these areas will be seemingly devoid of water or will have just a few inches covering them. Needless to say, no water, no fish. However, once the tide switches and begins to flood, these flats come alive with an abundance of marine life that was just buried in the nutrient-rich mud, or oyster or mussel beds. Predatory fish such as bonefish, redfish, permit, tarpon, and stripers know this and move up onto these flats, in the grasses or back under the mangrove roots, in search of a wide variety of marine life including crabs, shrimp, worms, and small baitfish. Anglers targeting these species must be keenly aware of these tidal influences in order to be successful. This is where very accurate tidal information acquired through official marine sources and experience on the water is a must. Wind also can have a strong influence on tides. A strong prolonged wind can literally hold back the tide in some narrow bays and creeks, sometimes causing the water to build. That same wind in the opposite direction can impede the approaching tide, empty a shallow bay, or keep a flat dry. If you fish these areas, it may take a number of visits before you begin to figure things out, but just think of the satisfaction you'll get out of it when you unravel the mystery. Another route is to hire an experienced guide from whom you can learn the area much more quickly.

To determine what the tidal flows will be for a certain date and time, there are a number of sources you can go to. Tidal information can often be found in your local newspapers in the weather section, but these usually only cover some of the more general areas and major inlets. Local tackle and bait shops often provide free printups of local tidal information for the season as a courtesy to their angling clientele. For tidal information covering more specific locations, you may need to use *Reed's Nautical Almanac* (see the appendix for Fly-Fishing Resources) for either the East or West Coast depending upon your location. *Reed's* provides thousands of points up and down each coast and can be very helpful as quick reference, although you will need to do some simple calculations. With the advent of the World Wide Web, those of us with access to a computer can quickly access tidal information for virtually anyplace on the globe (see the appendix). Sometimes this is all you'll need. However, many anglers fish tidal rivers, creeks, flats, and areas of backcountry that don't show up on these common sources. The only accurate way to determine the correct tidal flows is to spend time on the water. Then you'll know for sure and can jot down the correct tidal differences in your fishing diary, and you'll have it for future reference in planning your fishing. You may be surprised to find that tides in some areas may vary by a couple of hours from what you find in *Reed's* or on the Web. There's nothing worse than arriving at your targeted location only to find the tide is quitting and you'll have to wait perhaps two to three hours before things start happening again, or the flats are still dry because the tide hasn't risen yet.

Also keep in mind that tides advance by approximately one hour each day. So if you had a great outgoing tide yesterday, Saturday, at 6 P.M. and caught a ton of fish and wanted to try it again today, you would hit the same approximate tide at 7 P.M. (one hour later). Tides also repeat themselves approximately every two weeks. So to catch the same tide on another Saturday, you would need to return in two weeks at approximately 6 P.M.

Light

For certain species, light is an important consideration. Once settled into their summer patterns, striped bass and sea trout/weakfish in the mid-Atlantic and New England areas are primarily low-light or nocturnal feed-

Many predatory fish prefer low-light conditions. This is especially true for striped bass. Here the author holds a good upper Chesapeake bass taken during foggy conditions. This was a magical day with many bass caught and released during the morning.

ers, especially the big ones. With their large, specialized eyes and an efficient lateral line system for locating bait, bass and sea trout/weakfish are well adapted for feeding in security under the cover of darkness and low-light conditions. Anglers are not likely to do well seeking these species during daylight hours, especially during the summer months. I have fishing acquaintances who tell me that they're not doing well at all fly fishing along the beaches or the back bays. I eventually ask them when they are doing most of their fishing, and they almost always tell me during daylight hours. Many are surprised to learn that the most productive time to target these species is at night or at least during late-evening and early-morning hours under low-light conditions. Some are not willing to alter their schedules and continue not to catch fish. Others heed the advice and begin to experience marvelous fishing under the stars. If you haven't fished at night, you have to try it. It's a whole other experience. Visibility at night is a lot better than you would imagine. Lights from bridges, boats, and surrounding land structures reflect off the water and combine with the light from the moon and stars to create a tranquil, almost spiritual experience.

Safety concern: Before venturing out at night you should be very familiar with the areas you'll be fishing, especially when wading. Know the bottom structure, the weather, and the tides, and always have a fishing partner for safety reasons. It's also advisable to have a portable VHF radio and/or a cell phone along in case of emergencies.

At night, in the safety of darkness, fish usually move in closer to the beach or shore to feed. They are far less wary and won't be able to see you. No need to wade very far out in the surf. Stripers and trout will usually be feeding right in the suds. Jetty fishing will also be very productive as predatory fish corner the bait against the rocks. Even at night there's usually enough background light to see the boils and swirls of fish feeding. If you listen carefully, you may also hear the fish sipping or popping bait at the surface. In the Gulf states, fishing at night for specks and/or snook is also very productive. Bridge and dock lights tend to attract smaller baitfish, which in turn bring in the predatory fish. Even waters surrounded by fairly populated areas offer exceptional fishing under the stars for those anglers willing to venture a try. There's hardly any boat traffic and it's a very peaceful time to be on the water, making the fishing that much more rewarding.

Some of my best striper fishing has been during early mornings on semifoggy days. As soon as the fog lifted, the fish turned right off. Safety is first in these situations. Only venture out if you are totally familiar with the water you'll be fishing and you have a compass and/or a GPS if you're fishing from a boat or wading large, expansive areas. The fog could close in and get worse, stranding you on the water. Always put safety first.

Light, however, becomes an important component of success when sight casting to fish on the flats. Here, it doesn't pay to get up too early, because even if the fish are feeding on the flats it will be very difficult to see them. Ideally, when flats fishing for such species as bonefish, permit, tarpon, redfish, and snook, you want the sun to be up high and at your back to minimize surface glare so that the water in front of you is fully illuminated right to the bottom. A bonefish cruising the flats will be much easier to spot during bright light than with overcast skies. Even a partly cloudy day can cause problems. There's nothing more frustrating than spotting a beautiful bonefish, then getting ready to cast—only to lose sight of the fish at the last moment when a cloud temporarily blocks the sun. By the time the cloud passes you've usually lost your opportunity.

When trying to chum up some species like false albacore that are extremely sight-oriented, it's a good idea to wait until there is good bright light. Later in morning until midafternoon seems to be best: The sun is higher in the sky and provides optimum visibility for the albies to actually see the chum.

Water Clarity

The weather forecast was perfect for early-spring striper fishing on the upper Chesapeake Bay. The previous two days were clear and mild and free of any precipitation, and today was going to be a repeat. Upon arriving at the dock, I quickly discovered the bay was the color of coffee with floating debris—including some pieces the size of telephone poles—just about everywhere. The day's fishing was over before it began. What I failed to account for was the large amount of precipitation that had fallen four days earlier throughout the upper reaches of the watershed for the Susquehanna River in Pennsylvania more than 60 miles to the north. As the water flowed downstream, the Conowingo Dam just above the upper bay was releasing triple its normal flow. Not only was it foolhardy to try to fish, but I would have been risking my safety trying to navigate a boat through all the debris. The muddied waters fouled the fishing for at least 10 miles down the bay, and it would take several days of normal flow out of the dam to get the fishing back on track. Let me suggest that if you're faced with situations like this, first check water flows with the U.S. Geological Survey at www.usgs.gov. If they don't look good, plan an alternate location or stay home and get caught up on chores around the house until things improve.

Water clarity tends to improve the fishing, whereas turbid water (as in this case) tends to either turn most species off and/or make it nearly impossible to sight fish. Several years back, I had to make a business trip to Puerto Rico in February and thought it would be nice to treat myself to some redfishing in the Ten Thousand Islands of the Everglades along southwest Florida. I booked my guide and arrange for a stopover in Miami on my return trip to the States. My fly-fishing trip wound up being a bust, because of the effects of El Niño. High winds were whipping up the bottom of the shallow Gulf, and on incoming tides the turbid water would be sucked up and pulled back into the Glades, muddying up the water and reducing visibility even in the shallowest of waters to near zero.

Just as turbid water can ruin fishing, high water clarity can often result in great fishing opportunities. Pelagic speedsters like bonito and false albacore seek clearer waters because they hunt down their prey primarily by sight. Along the northeastern coast during late summer to midfall, some tremendous bonito and albacore fishing can be had after a nor'easter blows in clearer water. The effects of clearer water improving the albacore fishing can also be readily observed in the Cape Lookout area of North Carolina each year. Spending time on the water will enable you to record the weather conditions that can lead to both situations. You need to be aware of these conditions and know when they are occurring so you can plan accordingly.

Wind

As just mentioned above, nor'easters along the northeastern coast tend to improve the fishing, because they blow in clearer water—and lots of bait along with it. During these times it's classic Northeast surf fishing for stripers and blues at its best. The smaller baitfish are not strong swimmers, so they get carried by the strong shoreward-bound currents that are driven by the winds. Baitfish are literally driven right up on the beaches, where stripers and blues enjoy a feeding frenzy. Most times surf fishermen have no need to wade out into these treacherous waters. A short cast is all that's needed to be right in the middle of all the action. On a smaller scale, local wind conditions could cause similar phenomena in a bay, river, or estuary, trapping bait along a beach, river or sod bank, or edge of mangroves.

While high winds (15 to 20 mph) should be of concern to boaters, more importantly they should be adequately understood. In many cases it's not so much the wind that can cause danger to boaters, but rather the effects of the wind in developing and building wave action and currents. I fish frequently in my home waters along the New Jersey coast. With winds blowing 15 to 20 mph anywhere out of the northeast to the south, I would at least think twice about going out in my boat. Depending on how long it's been blowing, there could be waves of 4 feet and more making it unsafe to be out in an 18-foot boat. However, if those winds were instead blowing out of the west, they would tend to knock the waves and swells down, resulting in pretty calm and safe conditions near shore for about 2 or 3 miles. I've had clients cancel charters on these days only to enjoy some outstanding fishing right off the beaches. This past year, I had a similar experience albacore fishing at Cape Lookout, North Carolina. The morning of our first day, we had winds blowing out of the north at 20 to 25 mph. However, in that locale, north winds are blowing right off land, and we would essentially be fishing in the lee. What was also in our favor was that the north winds were helping flush large amounts of baitfish out of Beaufort Inlet to the waiting albies. The result was a windy day, manageable seas, and some great topwater action for albies. If my friend and I had stayed back at the Fishing Center, we would have missed a great time.

There's probably no place that's harder to hide from the effects of the wind than the flats in the Tropics. Fifteen, even 20 mph winds are considered normal. Trying to keep the wind and sun at your back for easier casting and visibility is the key. It was several years ago and I was bonefishing southern Abaco in the Bahamas. Unfortunately, the wind was relentless in blowing 25 to 35 mph around the clock. I found out the hard way that in this part of the Bahamas in March, there are usually strong winds that blow from east to west. Besides leading to very poor visibility to see cruising bonefish, the conditions also posed another interesting problem. You see, the southern portion of the island is cut with numerous creeks, shallow bays, and channels that run, as it happens, east and west. The wind was so strong and blowing so continuously that it was literally blowing the water in the east side of the island and seemingly just as quickly out the west side. The water never had a chance to stack up during high tide. In five days of fishing, I never saw the water even touch the edge of the mangroves, let alone reach way back inside. The only productive fishing that we could find was along the edges of the creeks, where we could fish the lee side of large, dense mangroves, giving us calmer and clearer water conditions where we could effectively sight fish.

Boat Traffic

As populations increase, so too will boat traffic. Sound is amplified under water. Just dropping a hatch cover or stepping off a casting platform is all that it might take to put a school of bonefish on the alert some 200 feet or more away. If fish are so sensitive to those minor sounds, how do you imagine they feel about someone running an outboard over their heads? This may be a mind-blowing revelation for many folks, but boat motor noise, even an 8-horsepower outboard at idle, is not good for fishing unless you're trolling for pelagics in the open ocean. People blowing up on and through school stripers has ruined more fishing opportunities for me than I care to remember. Believe me, these are not just joyriders, but include head boats, boats fishing with conventional tackle, and yes, I'm sad to say . . . many fellow fly fishermen. At least the fly fishermen wave a pleasant hello, but it doesn't help. They still can turn off the fishing for everyone, including themselves. The worst part is, they'll never know until they try to approach fish under stealth mode. If they were to try it a few times, they would quickly change their ways, because they would see their fishing improve dramatically.

It's becoming more and more difficult to find out-of-the-way places that have minimal boat traffic. If you can find these places, you are indeed lucky. But if you're like most anglers, you've got to learn when to fish the most productive spots when there's the least amount of boat traffic. The best time is obviously on a weekday, when most folks are working. Midweek is usually best, since things will quiet down for a few days, giving the fish time to get back into their normal feeding routine. If you're like me and have a full-time job, you may only be able to do this a few times during the year by taking a vacation day or what I like to call a "mental health day." Other great times to avoid heavy traffic and enjoy some outstanding fishing are early in the morning—one hour before to one hour after sunrise—and at night. You'll be quite surprised at how the same locations that are nonproductive during the day with all the boat traffic come alive during the night and/or early-morning hours. It may require some rescheduling, but if you can do it on occasion, the fishing usually makes it worthwhile.

Availability of Bait

As the saying goes . . . *Find the bait and you'll find the fish.* This saying is very true, especially during the spring and fall migrations up and down the East Coast and throughout its estuaries. In open water, bluefish and stripers will be chasing schools of bunker and herring. Locate the surface action and you'll be in business. Silversides, herring, shrimp, crabs, and

Spend time on the water and explore its mysteries. You never know where it may lead and what magical moments you may encounter.

other sorts of bait will be moving into the tidal rivers, inlets, and back bays to spawn and take up residence for the season. Here fly fishing from shore, wading, or taking out a canoe or kayak can be very productive. Spending time on the water scouting and talking to local fishermen and folks at bait and tackle shops can give you an early sign that fish are moving into the local waters. When I refer to "fisherman, " I mean anyone fishing with a rod. Early in the season bait fishermen are usually the first to begin hooking up. If they're catching fish, then the fish are at least beginning to move in. This may be your signal to start working the waters in the area with a fly.

As mentioned above, baitfish are attracted to dock and bridge lights at night, and they in turn attract predatory fish. No dock in southwest Florida is complete unless it's equipped with a "snook light." Commercial trawlers can also attract lots of predatory fish. Shrimp trawlers operate all along the southeastern and Gulf coastlines. The by-catch that they discard periodically when they bring their nets in attracts a host of predatory fish. One of the most common gamefish that can be found trailing behind trawlers is the false albacore, commonly referred to as bonito in Florida for some strange reason. Albies are dynamite on a fly rod. Large jacks can also be found following trawlers and are fantastic to catch on a fly rod. Even clamming boats off New Jersey attract stripers. Tie on a good clam imitation and you're in business.

Up and down the East Coast, late summer and early fall sees the beginning of the end-of-season migration of baitfish out of the back bays and rivers. Baitfish usually use times of full moon, with their extra-high tides, to ride the tide out into the salt water. These are times of plenty. The large concentrations of baitfish attract gamefish by the droves. Striped bass, false albacore, bonito, weakfish, bluefish, and Spanish mackerel feast on the abundant bait. Find the baitfish and you'll often find a variety of gamesters enjoying the bounty at the same time. The action can usually be found in and around the mouths of rivers and inlets and along the beaches where they dump their cargo of bait into the ocean. A day or two can make all the difference. Fly fishermen wait all year for this action, so if you want to get your share of magical moments, you'll need to spend time on the water.

It's important to mention that proper use of the strategies covered in this book will not happen unless you spend time on the water. You can read all you want about fishing, but you'll never have a solid reference point unless you've actually been there and done that. It's that simple. I believe this is what can make fly fishing so incredibly fascinating for some and so frustrating for others. If you're looking for a sport where you're successful all the time . . . you've come to the wrong place.

To be successful in saltwater fly fishing requires a keen understanding of the seven strategies covered in this book and their application on the water over time. It will be up to you to spend time on the water and apply them in the various fishing scenarios that you'll likely encounter. As you do, keep in mind that many of these situations may present new challenges. Nobody has all the answers, and nobody can be successful all the time. In the short term this may be frustrating, but if you persevere, over the long term your rate of improvement will steadily increase, as will your success and enjoyment of fly fishing's intricacies. It helps to keep in mind that this is just part of a continuous learning process. Just think how good you'll feel each time you unravel another of fly fishing's mysteries. Hopefully, you'll learn to enjoy solving these mysteries and realize that catching fish in the process is an added bonus.

STRATEGY 3—SPEND TIME ON THE WATER

There's no substitute for time spent on the water. If you don't spend time on the water, you'll never realize your fullest potential, since you won't know enough about the where, when, and how of fishing salt waters. Become more knowledgeable and increase your odds of success by...
- Observing and learning while on the water.
- Discovering the secrets of where to fish.
- Developing knowledge and skills on how to spot fish.
- Learning the effects of the following and determining when best to fish:

> Water temperature.
> Tidal stage.
> Light.
> Water clarity.
> Wind.
> Boat traffic.
> Availability of bait.

STRATEGY

USE THE
RIGHT FLY

U sing the right fly for saltwater fly fishing is like using the right tool to
do a job. A coping saw is not going to work at driving an eight-penny
nail into a piece of wood. A hammer is needed. On the other hand, a hammer and chisel may cut a fine piece of wooden molding, but it will take a
while, and it won't look pretty when it's done. However, a coping saw with
its fine teeth and subtle blade will follow the contours of the wooden
molding and do an excellent job in cutting it. Just as no one tool is right for
all jobs, no one fly is right for all fishing situations. And just as a carpenter

would carry an assortment of select tools around his waist for the variety of jobs he may encounter, so too should a saltwater fly fisher carry a select variety of different flies.

I was striper fishing in early November off the northern Jersey coast with my friend Rick Bender when we encountered large schools of surface-feeding stripers. The prevalent bait in the fall is baby bunker. We each had a rod rigged and ready with a bunker imitation. I positioned the boat up-wind and upcurrent from the school, and as the boat drifted quietly along, we found ourselves surrounded by the feeding fish. This was going to be easy, we thought, licking our chops with anticipation. Eagerly, we made re-peated casts into the school—without even a touch. Rick was fishing with a Teeny 350 and finally hooked up, but then found it difficult to hook up again. Something was drastically wrong. How could it be possible that with all the hundreds of fish that were actively feeding, they were refusing our offerings? It was evident that the fish were telling us something. They did-n't want something big, so I tied on a small 1½-inch rainbait imitation made from craft fur. On the very first cast, my line came tight immediately. Voilà! The right fly for the job. Using the right fly may not matter much in some fishing situations, but in others it may mean the difference between fishing and catching.

CHARACTERISTICS

There are four basic characteristics for any fly: profile, color, buoyancy, and breathability.

Perhaps the most significant is profile. The term *profile* encompasses length, depth, and width of a fly and seems to give a more complete and holistic description of a fly than just size or length. The reason why a fly's profile is most important is because it's usually what makes the first im-pression to the fish. If the fly is approximately the same size and shape as the baitfish they're feeding on, usually you're in business. In many circum-stances, gamefish will only see a fly in silhouette backlit by the sun or nightlit sky. Flies fished deeper in the water column will lose most of their color as sunlight is filtered out and absorbed. Gamefish will then depend more on their lateral line system to detect and interpret prey. Profile is therefore the most important consideration.

When considering profile, the fly's length is probably the most impor-tant dimension. It should generally be the same approximate size as the bait you're trying to imitate. This can vary widely for different geographic areas and for different seasons of the year in the same areas. Size does matter. Menhaden or bunker, for example, along the northeastern coast can range from 3 or 4 inches for baby bunker to 12 inches or more for large adult bunker. Many times bluefish and stripers are keyed into the specific length of the baitfish they are pursuing. An inch too long or short and they may not take your offering. It's always a good idea to have several different profiles of the same fly to cover a wide range of possible fishing situations. While bunker may be a good example of a very large-profile variation that can occur for the same baitfish, more subtle profile differences can also occur for smaller baitfish like sand eels, glass minnows, pilchards, and silversides. Although these differences may only be in fractions of an inch and be far less obvious to us, don't underestimate their significance. Size does matter, even if it's on a lesser scale.

Other physical characteristics such as body depth and width of baitfish may also be important. For deeper-bodied baitfish like bunker, pilchards, or butterfish, a deep-profiled or spread fly will do an excellent job simulating this important characteristic. Mullet, on the other hand, have a

Hooked up in South Andros. Using the right fly is especially critical when fishing the gin-clear flats of the Bahamas for bonefish and permit.

wider or fatter cigarlike profile. Bob Popovics's Silicone Mullet pattern is effective in imitating this standout characteristic. With smaller baitfish, there may be a tendency to overlook or even underestimate the importance of these same characteristics because of their size. Most gamefish have keen eyesight and can detect slight differences in a fly's characteristics, even on a much smaller scale. Flies simulating or imitating silversides should have a slender profile, while sand eels and needlefish should be quite thin on average.

Profile is also an important characteristic when imitating or simulating other types of bait, including shrimp and crabs. When pursuing one of my favorite species, the bonefish, I generally use a much larger shrimp pattern when fishing in the Bahamas than when fishing other Caribbean waters. This, however, may have more to do with the size of the bonefish. In my experience, bones in the Bahamas and Florida are on average considerably larger than their Caribbean counterparts. I've also found that big bones usually prefer big bait. There's another advantage to using larger flies when bonefishing—you'll be able to see your fly more easily. This is key in determining where your fly is in relationship to the fish so you'll know when to retrieve and when to set the hook after the bone has sucked in your fly.

Color, including flash, is next in importance. In many situations your fly will need to pass the profile test before a gamefish will even consider committing. Once it moves in, it will be taking an even closer look. The fly's color will be an important factor in determining whether it gets snatched up or not. In clearer waters a fly's color may need to closely duplicate the color of the natural bait, while in more turbid water bright colors and a lot of flash may be needed to attract a strike. False albacore, for example, have excellent eyesight and can detect the slightest color variation. I've fished for them in situations where they were highly selective, taking only silverside imitations with just a little chartreuse on the top wing. If you had the exact same fly in every detail but were missing the chartreuse, you wouldn't get a take.

For bonefish, it's always highly recommended that the color of your flies closely match the color of the bottom in the areas you'll be fishing. For light sandy bottoms, white, tan, or otherwise very translucent colors generally work best. Darker mottled bottoms interspersed with turtle grass may call for darker-colored flies in tans, browns, greens, and so on. The reason for this is that the baitfish's and crustaceans' natural protective camouflage mechanism mimics the color of their surrounding environment so predators will find them harder to spot. However, if the natural colors aren't working, it's always a good idea to try a color combination that is totally different from any natural.

Fishing in low-light and turbid-water conditions, on the other hand, is usually a black-fly event. This seems totally illogical, but a dark fly offers the greatest contrast and will therefore stand out and be more noticeable to predatory fish that feed at night like snook and striped bass. Black is also an excellent color choice when fishing white water in the surf for the same reason.

Buoyancy is third on my list of importance overall. It is a key factor in determining the type of movement the fly will have when it's not being retrieved in the water and where in the water column it will be most effective. On one end of the spectrum, you have weighted flies using primarily Clouser-type weighted eyes or coneheads that cause flies to quickly drop or sink when not retrieved or in between retrieves, giving flies an up-and-down jiglike motion. On the other, you have poppers that float on the surface and sliders and other flies like Crease Flies and the Clouser Floating Minnow that float in the surface. In between, there are flies that are more neutrally buoyant, such as a Deceiver; these suspend and sink very slowly in a delightful tease.

Large weighted flies are often designed and used for fishing deeper in the water column for species like striped bass. These weighted flies, used in conjunction with sinking lines, will help the entire system sink more uniformly down to where the bigger fish like to hang. However, less heavily weighted flies can be effectively fished within 2 to 4 feet of the surface with the aid of floating or intermediate fly lines and a faster retrieve to keep them up in the water column when fish are feeding at or just below the surface. Fishing 2- to 3-inch Clouser-type silversides in this fashion is a common way to take false albacore along the mid-Atlantic and New England coasts. Although bonefish are generally targeted while cruising shallow flats in water of 3 feet or less, a host of bonefish fly patterns use lead or bead-chain eyes to create the same jiglike up-and-down motion. These weighted flies are especially effective because when the angler stops his retrieve, the fly settles to the bottom much the way a crab or shrimp would attempt to hide from a predator. The amount and type of wing material that the fly is tied with will also have an impact on the fly's buoyancy. A fly with a heavy upper wing of deer hair, for example, will be more buoyant than, say, a fly with a heavy wing of marabou or synthetic Super Hair. The wing in this case acts somewhat like a parachute and slows down the descent of the fly. This can be a very desirable feature in some fishing situations. By varying the weight that you add to a fly and the amount and type of wing material, you can vary the fly's action and fish at different depths more effectively.

It's important to point out that as a general rule, the weight and wing material added to a fly should primarily be used to create the desired action and should not be used as the principal means to cause the fly to sink. Use sinking lines of varying densities for that purpose.

Breathability is a term that I think best describes the natural lifelike subtle undulating motion that some flies have, which will often entice even the most finicky of fish. It's a close fourth on my list of most important characteristics. Both natural and synthetic materials like marabou and Sparkle Flash have high breathability, while bucktail and Krystal Flash have medium breathability. Those flies using mostly rigid or semirigid materials like epoxy, silicone, or foam would have low breathability. A traditional Lefty's Deceiver would be an example of a fly with medium breathability. Take that same fly, add a flash tail with Flashabou, and use soft marabou instead of a collar of bucktail, and you now have the same fly with high breathability. When fishing in very clear waters like a bonefish flat where the fish will have an opportunity to really give the fly a thorough look-over, flies that have more breathability will often be substantially more effective. It's simple—with all that movement, they look like they're really alive when being retrieved or when at rest. On the other hand, a Dupree epoxy Spoon Fly has low breathability, but is still a very effective fly in many shallow-water situations because of its action. Just ask a redfisherman.

Here's a fishing situation that may be a good example of how all four of these characteristics can strongly influence your angling success. It was early spring, and I was catch-and-release fishing for stripers in the upper Chesapeake Bay. The spring spawning migration coincides with a large spawning run of herring. Wakes, boils, the spattering of bait clouds from the water, and the occasional surface explosion indicated that stripers were gorging themselves on medium to large herring on the flats. I was hoping to take them on topwater poppers so their strikes would be completely visible. They would follow and wake, but would not commit. Switching to a white deer hair slider, I made several casts, only to be disappointed again. I could clearly see several stripers following the fly while I retrieved it slightly under the surface, but when I stopped the retrieve and the fly slowly floated to the surface, they would abruptly cut off their attack. Reaching into my fly box, I pulled out one of my own favorite patterns . . . a Pretender Herring. I find this pattern especially effective because I can vary the color and length to match the "hatch." Tied flashback style with blue-green Sparkle Flash and a large epoxy head, the fly has high attracting power and breathability, and the slight forward weight causes it to dip slightly in a slow tantalizing tease. Tying on an 8- to 10-inch Pretender Herring, I laid out a long cast. I imme-diately began retrieving the fly with fast, rapid strips to keep it up near the surface to attract some attention. A wake appeared behind the fly and moved up, but the fish wouldn't strike. I paused the retrieve; the fly dipped downward with its hackles and flash top undulating in their tantalizing dance. Suddenly there was a flash just under the surface followed by a large boil and my line came tight to a feisty striper. This scenario was repeated again and again over the course of the next two days, accounting for hun-dreds of stripers being caught and released.

It's important to note that in this situation, all four basic characteristic of a fly were essential for the overall effectiveness of the pattern. The pro-file and color were most critical to initially interest the stripers. The slightly nonbuoyant fly created with the epoxy head—causing the fly to dip and sink slowly—really turned on the stripers in this situation, and the high breathability created with the saddle hackles, Flashabou, and flash top sealed the stripers' fate. It was simply irresistible.

But the story doesn't end there. Three days later, I went to the exact same area to fish the late afternoon and evening. As anticipated, the stripers were there and were showing themselves with surface boils dis-guised slightly by a 1-foot chop. I figured, why mess around with success, and tied on the same Pretender Herring. Cast after cast failed to take a fish. A little puzzled, I began experimenting with different color combinations using the same pattern. Nothing. Then I tried an 8- to 10-inch Half & Half Herring pattern, followed by poppers, sliders, chartreuse-and-white Clousers, and on, and on. Still nothing. I was getting a little frustrated when I remembered seeing smaller 3- to 4-inch herring spraying from the water on occasion three days previous. I tied on a 3-inch all-white Clouser and gave it a try. Within the next hour, I took 12 fish between 8 and 15 pounds all on that same fly. This second scenario again illustrates how profile, color, and buoyancy were critical to angling success. Breathability was, I believe, less critical in this situation because the waters were a little rougher and the stripers had to decide to take more quickly.

Every saltwater fly has these four characteristics of profile, color, buoyancy, and breathability. The wise fly tier takes each characteristic into account when crafting a fly. Each has a purpose, and each is important in determining the eventual effectiveness of the fly in catching fish. There is, however, a fifth characteristic—translucency. This has gained much popularity in recent years with the development of a variety of synthetic tying materials like Ultra Hair, epoxy, silicone, Corsair, and so forth. These new materials come in a wide variety of colors, but allow distorted light to pass through, thereby being translucent. Many baitfish possess a translucent appearance. Flies tied with these materials can take on an uncanny lifelike appearance and add a whole new dimension of illusion to the flies we tie. Although technically not translucent, tying sparse flies with bucktail (for example) is another way to give the illusion of translucency. These characteristics are blended together in endless variations to create three types of flies: simulators, imitators, and attractors.

SIMULATORS

By and large, most anglers fish simulators most of the time. They're not intended to be an exact imitation. Instead, simulators are flies that essentially can simulate or mimic any of a variety of baitfish. This is important since anglers often may not know exactly what bait is available or what bait the fish will prefer. With a simulator, anglers increase their odds of success. The two most famous fly-tying styles for simulators are Bob Clouser's Deep Minnow and Lefty Kreh's Deceiver. They have probably caught more different species and perhaps more fish in total than all other flies combined. They can be tied to mimic many different baitfish, including silversides, bunker, mullet, herring, sand eels, small shad, sardines, and pilchards, by simply varying the profile and coloration to simulate those of the baitfish commonly found in the waters you fish. An all-white or chartreuse-over-white Clouser or Deceiver with a blue-green back and some flash could simulate most of these baitfish in many situations.

The weighted eyes or cone used on a Clouser or a Bob Popovics Jiggy Fly causes the fly to drop sharply like a jig when paused on the retrieve.

This darting up-and-down motion is very effective, especially when the fish are working deeper in the water column. Lefty's Deceiver, on the other hand, is almost neutrally buoyant when in the water, but its soft saddle hackles create breathability and a lifelike motion when the fly is paused on the retrieve that is irresistible to many fish. Another great simulator that was recently developed by Capt. Joe Bladoes is the Crease Fly. The Crease Fly gets its name from the use of closed-cell foam, which makes the fly buoyant, causing it to float just under or flat on the surface. These flies are extremely effective when fish are feeding at or near the surface. The Crease Fly tied with a tail of medium- to high-breathability material floats in a subtle, tantalizing way, right in front of where the fish are feeding. False albacore, stripers, blues, and a host of other fish can't seem to eat them fast enough. Just select a fly of the approximate size of the baitfish. While each of these flies is extremely effective for catching fish under certain circumstances, they are tied to emphasize one or more of the five characteristics.

Fly fishers who are often successful in their angling efforts have a variety of simulators in their personal arsenal to impersonate the baitfish

Some of the bait that needs to be simulated are quite large, such as this 16-inch herring that was actually caught on a 3" fly.

Whoever said size doesn't matter was lying. Greg Mentzer with a large striper that succumbed to a large Half & Half Herring pattern. If you want to catch large stripers, use very large flies. (Photo: Greg and Carol Mentzer)

they're likely to encounter in the waters they fish. While I personally enjoy tying new fly patterns and have found some to be highly effective in catching fish, you have to be careful not to get too caught up with tying and fishing every newfangled fly variation that comes along. Much of our fly-tying time is limited, plus many of these flies are designed more for catching anglers than fish. Many have not been time-proven. My suggestion is to find several fly designs that work, then tie them with different profiles, color variations, and perhaps buoyancy. These are my go-to patterns that are tried and true.

Years ago I began systematizing my approach to tying flies when I planned a bonefishing trip to the Bahamas. During previous trips, I learned that out of all the wild variations of flies that I tied and brought along, only a small number of simulator shrimp-type patterns caught fish with a high degree of consistency. I knew from these experiences that these fly patterns worked. Now, to take only flies of a single fly pattern, all with the same profile, color, and buoyancy, bonefishing would be foolish. Waters for bonefishing to the inexperienced may seem to vary only slightly in depth and bottom color, but these subtle differences are often critical to the angler's success. Most often, a fly's color needs to closely match the prevalent color of the bottom. Light bottom, light fly. Dark bottom, dark fly. Also, a shallow flat's depth of 18 inches versus 8 inches when bonefishing may not seem that significant, but to a northeastern coast angler it may be comparable to fishing in water that is 8 feet versus only 2 feet deep. First, you have to get the fly down into the fish's strike zone, and second, you don't want to alarm or spook the fish during the presentation. Another consideration is profile. Bonefish in the Bahamas usually prefer a bigger meal since they generally run larger than the bones in the Caribbean.

Rather than tying a wide range of fly patterns to be prepared for these variations of water depth, bottom color, and bait size, I narrowed the field down to "the vital few" fly patterns that I knew would work, and then just varied these in profile, color, translucency, and buoyancy for the conditions I expected. I call the bonefish pattern variation I developed a Bam-Boozle, since it is so effective in tricking bonefish that in no time—*bam!*—you're hooked up. I would tie a series of these in 2, 4, and 6 hook sizes in colors ranging from white to white and pink, light tan, and perhaps olive and tan with Sparkle Flash. This gave me the profile, color variation, and breathability I needed. For each size and color variation, I would tie several with large brass or silver bead-chain or small lead eyes for deeper water of, say, 2 to 3 feet, then several with medium bead-chain eyes for 1 to 2 feet of water, and finally several with no weighted eyes at all for very skinny water of 1 foot or less and those delicate situations. With a fly box filled with Bam-Boozles, I was set for almost any situation.

Although this example was for bonefish, I apply the same approach for flies that I routinely use in my home water along the mid-Atlantic, the Delaware and Chesapeake Bays. The Pretender streamer pattern variation that I tie is simple and effective. With slight variations in profile and color, including flash, I can simulate baby bunker, mullet, herring, shad, silversides, and other baitfish with just this one pattern. This eliminates the need to have to spend a lot of time at the vise tying, the need to carry a ton of different fly patterns around, and the need to spend a lot of time on the water sorting through the endless patterns trying to figure out which one will likely work. Simulators can simplify the fly selection process and let you get on with the task at hand: catching fish.

IMITATORS

While some simulators may do a pretty good job replicating some bait, imitator fly patterns are designed to match specific bait in all manner of detail. This is matching the bait at its finest for fishing in salt waters. Imitators often require more exact tying materials and techniques to imitate the bait precisely. Duplicating a bait's profile and color becomes critical when tying imitators, but the rewards may be well worth the effort from both an artistic and a fish-catching perspective. Numerous anglers fishing for sea trout or weakfish along the Jersey coast and back bays swear that they actually catch more fish using Bob Popovics's Ultra Shrimp than they do fishing with live grass shrimp. That's simply amazing when you think about it. Bob is arguably the most innovative fly tier we have today. Using some rather nontraditional materials like Ultra Hair, five-minute epoxy, and silicone, Bob has created a wide assortment of highly realistic translucent imitators that includes such flies as the Ultra Shrimp mentioned above, the Surf Candy, and the Shady Lady Squid. Carl Richards and Glen Mikkleson tie extremely realistic crab imitations that look like they could walk right off the tying table.

The imitators mentioned above look amazingly lifelike out of the water just as they do in the water. There are, however, many other imitator patterns that are most realistic when wet or submerged in water. For example, variations of Lefty's Deceiver and Bob Clouser's Deep Minnow can be, and often are, tied with attention to exacting detail of many different baitfish. With the use of Ultra Hair, the Albie Clouser, for example, does a great job imitating translucent silversides and has been highly effective in taking false albacore, while a Spread Deceiver doubles as a bunker. Smaller flies tied with craft fur and sparse amounts of flash material look pretty good out of the water, but when submerged the synthetic craft fur gives a true-to-life translucency to the fly. A Glass Minnow really looks like a glass minnow. Besides its amazing translucency, craft fur is extremely supple, giving even the smallest of flies like a rainbait imitation high breathability and lifelike action.

I've put the craft fur rainbait imitation to the test a number of times while fishing along the Outer Banks of North Carolina. We would often chum up false albacore if breaking fish were scarce. If you've ever seen a false albacore up close, you would be sure to notice its huge eyes. In clear water, these green speedsters have incredible eyesight and can detect even the slightest difference between a natural rainbait and an imitator. We commonly use small amounts of rainbait to bring the albies up and within close

False albacore can be very selective. Be prepared with various sized silverside and rainbait imitators. The author with a beautiful albie caught while fishing the Cape Lookout area of North Carolina.

casting range of the boat. It's an awesome sight watching 30 or more of these beautiful and powerful pelagic speedsters right next to your boat and often just a rod's length away. The trick is to get a small rainbait imitation of just 1¼ to 1½ inches to float along in the chum and hope an albie snatches it up. The whole time you get to watch the show with your heart pounding as the albies come flying in to pick off the rainbait chum. If you don't have an exact match you can often watch an albie come flying in at top speed, slam on the brakes, eyeball your offering, and scoot off because it sees something unnatural. The craft fur rainbait imitation is so good that usually all you will see is albies flashing through the chum; next thing you know your line has come tight and your drag is screaming . . . "See ya!"

Some bait with silvery sides and dark backs, like herring, sardines, shad, and pilchards, are for the most part easy to imitate. However, accurate imitators of bait like bunker, silversides, crabs, and shrimp that possess a lot of color variations are more difficult and time-consuming to tie. For many of you, this may represent a challenge that you relish; you attain deep personal satisfaction when you pluck your creation from the maw of your quarry. For others it may be just a necessity to deal with in getting the job done. In either case, imitators can be very effective for many different species of fish at different times.

While to some anglers, imitators may look like a surefire way of catching fish most of the time, this is often not the case. One of the primary differences between fishing fresh and salt waters is the enormous volume of bait that salt waters can contain in different areas at different times. For a fish to find your imitator fly in these situations would be like trying to find your friend's car in a parking lot filled with cars of the same make, model, and color—an arduous task. Using exact imitations in situations when there is a lot of the same bait in the area you are fishing is often very ineffective since the fly can get lost among all the naturals. Sometimes in these situations using an imitator that is slightly different from the original will dramatically improve your hook-ups. No doubt you would quickly find your friend's car if it was the only car with a bold white stripe down the roof.

ATTRACTORS

As the name implies, attractors are designed first to attract or get the attention of predatory fish, then to entice a strike, many times in situations where they would not normally do so. There are three primary methods of crafting flies to attract fish: noise, color/flash, and vibration.

SIMULATORS

(All flies tied by the author unless otherwise noted.)

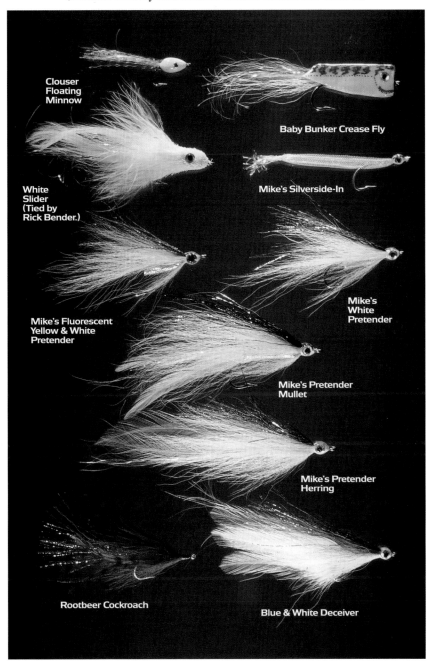

Clouser
Floating
Minnow

Baby Bunker Crease Fly

White
Slider
(Tied by
Rick Bender.)

Mike's Silverside-In

Mike's
White
Pretender

Mike's Fluorescent
Yellow & White
Pretender

Mike's Pretender
Mullet

Mike's Pretender
Herring

Rootbeer Cockroach

Blue & White Deceiver

SIMULATORS

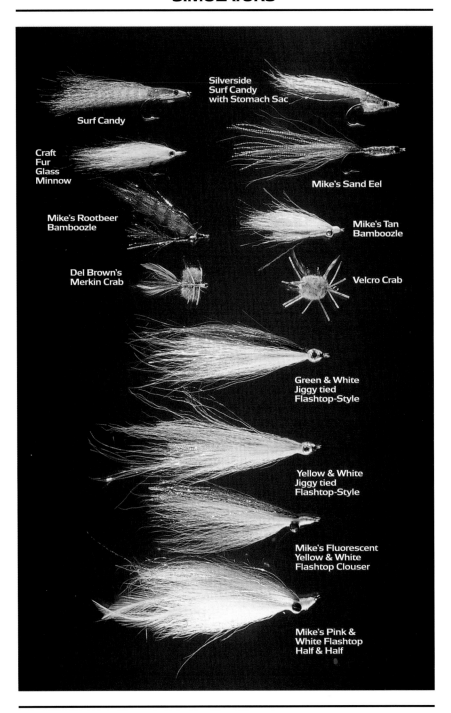

Surf Candy

Silverside
Surf Candy
with Stomach Sac

Craft
Fur
Glass
Minnow

Mike's Sand Eel

Mike's Rootbeer
Bamboozle

Mike's Tan
Bamboozle

Del Brown's
Merkin Crab

Velcro Crab

Green & White
Jiggy tied
Flashtop-Style

Yellow & White
Jiggy tied
Flashtop-Style

Mike's Fluorescent
Yellow & White
Flashtop Clouser

Mike's Pink &
White Flashtop
Half & Half

IMITATORS

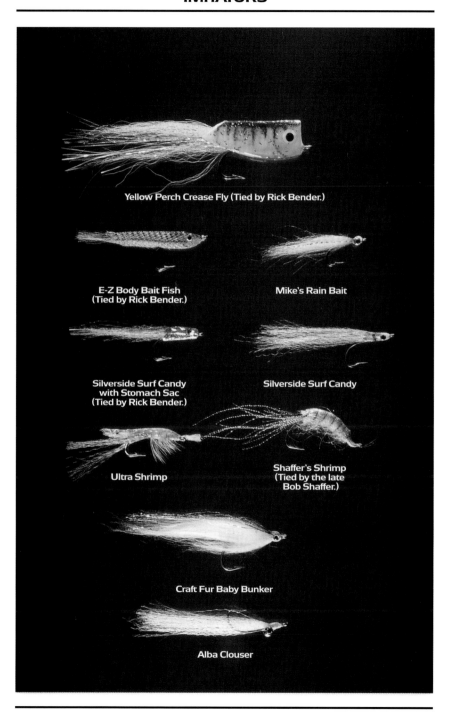

Yellow Perch Crease Fly (Tied by Rick Bender.)

E-Z Body Bait Fish
(Tied by Rick Bender.)

Mike's Rain Bait

Silverside Surf Candy
with Stomach Sac
(Tied by Rick Bender.)

Silverside Surf Candy

Ultra Shrimp

Shaffer's Shrimp
(Tied by the late
Bob Shaffer.)

Craft Fur Baby Bunker

Alba Clouser

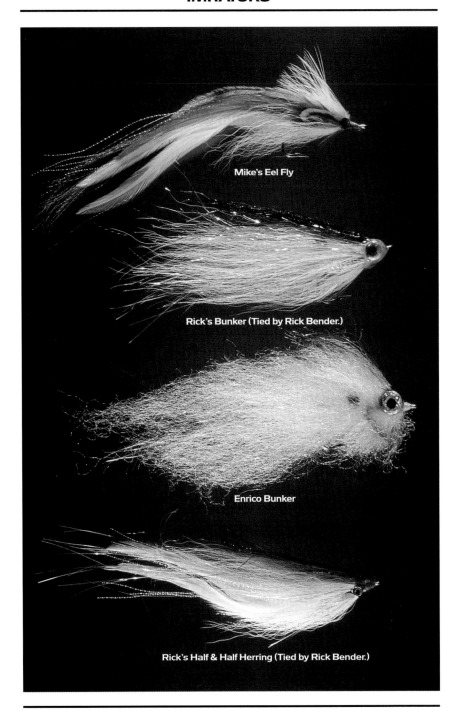

Mike's Eel Fly

Rick's Bunker (Tied by Rick Bender.)

Enrico Bunker

Rick's Half & Half Herring (Tied by Rick Bender.)

Bob's Banger

Rick's Goo-Goo Eyed Slider with Rattle Eyes (Tied by Rick Bender.)

Rick's Rattle Crease Fly (Tied by Rick Bender.)

Silver Crease Fly

Baby Crease Fly (Tied by Rick Bender.)

Clouser Floating Minnow (Tied by Rick Bender.)

Gartside Gurgler

Red & White Slider (Tied by Rick Bender.)

Yellow Perch Slab Fly (Tied by Rick Bender.)

ATTRACTORS

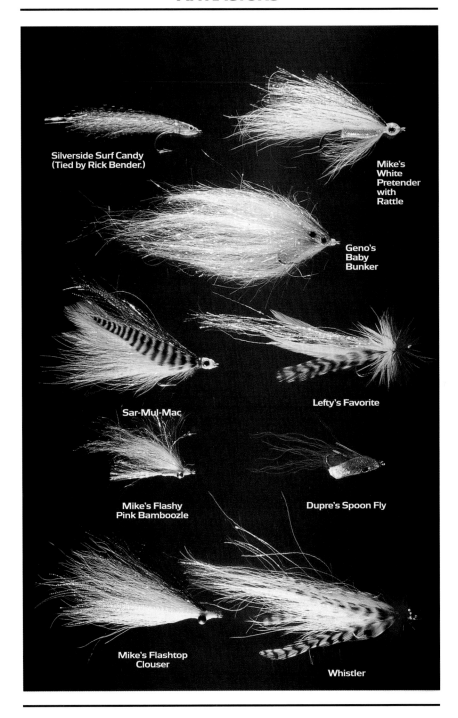

Silverside Surf Candy
(Tied by Rick Bender.)

Mike's
White
Pretender
with
Rattle

Geno's
Baby
Bunker

Sar-Mul-Mac

Lefty's Favorite

Mike's Flashy
Pink Bamboozle

Dupre's Spoon Fly

Mike's Flashtop
Clouser

Whistler

Author's wife, Patty, playing a bonefish while wading along Ambergris Cay, Belize.

The author with a spring striper from the flats of Barnegat Bay, New Jersey.

Hooked up off Thomas Point Light, Chesapeake Bay, Maryland.

Noise is probably the most recognizable method of attracting fish to strike your fly. Surface flies immediately come to mind, especially poppers. Poppers can be extremely effective under certain circumstances. The noise and splashing may call fish's attention to your fly; they'll think it's a wounded or distressed baitfish. The use of surface flies is often very effective when fish are actively feeding at the surface. Baitfish are splashing and going crazy trying to get away from the predatory fish below. Most of the time all you'll need to do is toss your surface fly out into all the commotion, strip it a few times to make some noise, and *pow!* . . . you're hooked up. Poppers are also useful in locating fish that may be in the area but are not interested in the ordinary run-of-the-mill fly. Noise travels farther in water, so the use of surface flies, especially ones that make a big commotion like Bob's Banger, can be very effective in covering a lot of surface water to find where the fish are located. Capt. Frank Granneri, who guides in the back bays surrounding Atlantic City, New Jersey, is known to fish exclusively with poppers for striped bass, weakfish, and bluefish. From late afternoon until dusk, Frank moves from location to location, having his clients cast to likely holding spots along the many islands and creeks. Predatory fish waiting in ambush can't seem to resist the inviting chugs, splashes, and gurgles and readily pounce on poppers cast in their vicinity.

Other more subtle surface/subsurface attractors including slider-type flies like Lou Tabory's Snake Fly, Jack Gartside's Gurgler, Bob Clouser's Floating Minnow, and Capt. Joe Bladoes's Crease Fly can be especially effective in soliciting strikes from a wide range of gamefish. While the designs of these flies may vary slightly, they have one thing in common—at times, fish can't seem to refuse them. The lure of Lou's Snake Fly, while subtle, becomes quite irresistible as the fly slips, slides, and pulsates through the surface film of the water like the action of an impaired baitfish. It works excitingly well on aggressively surface-feeding stripers and bluefish, just as it often can on fish that are more secretive and wary, like a redfish that is working the shallows of a quiet flat. Crease Flies are slightly different in their design. With the wide-profile foam, they float on their side and don't appear to work properly when compared to the other poppers and sliders. This feature is exactly what makes them so effective in many situations when fish are working just below or at the surface. In fact, they seem to work best when just lying on their side or when given just a few short pulls. A pulsating and quivering Crease Fly seems to attract predatory fish just like a helpless baitfish. Stripers, bluefish, and false albacore really eat them up.

Carol Mentzer and guide Capt. Sarah Gardner Horsley (Flat-Out Charters) show off a nice fat albert that attacked an attractor pattern that was larger and flashier than the abundant naturals. (Photo: Greg and Carol Mentzer)

There are many other attractor fly patterns that are fished within the water column. Attractor flies that have bright colors and a wide pushy profile that pushes water or create vibrations as they're retrieved include the Sea Ducer and Dan Blanton's Whistler. These types of flies are often effective in water with low clarity or visibility. Yellow and red Sea Ducers are longtime favorites for anglers fishing the mangrove backcountry for snook and redfish. The tiny vibrations sent out by the fly as it's retrieved are picked up by the well-developed lateral line system of these fish, which aids them in finding food even when they may not see it. Another effective color combo is a Whistler tied with chartreuse saddle hackles, a heavily tied black collar, and a lot of flash.

The true test of these and other flies is how well they work on the water. I was sight fishing in the Ten Thousand Islands area of the Everglades for snook and redfish. We were working inside a very shallow cove. Unfortunately, there were so many mullet that they disturbed the water as we approached, muddying it up to something that looked like chocolate milk. Jim Nickerson, a terrific guide, was poling us out of the roiled mess, I thought I spotted a large redfish tail that came up near the surface, just 30 feet or so off the left side of the boat, but vanished in the muck. I took a cast anyway to be on the safe side, but was not very optimistic. If the fish was there and I couldn't see the fly, how in the world would the fish see it? After I let the fly sink a bit, it quickly disappeared. I gave a few short quick strips when to my disbelief, out of the mud came the head of a good-sized redfish that promptly sucked in my fly. In this case I think the redfish felt the fly and as it closed in, the bright color and contrasting black collar enabled the redfish to finally find my offering.

Most attractor patterns are flies tied with a lot of flash. Such flies stand out from the crowd and get attention because they are immediately viewed as being different from all the other baitfish in the area. Liberace, dressed in his flashy sequin outfit and ostentatious jewelry, called attention to himself and clearly stood out in a crowd. He couldn't help but be noticed. The concept of a flashy attractor pattern should be no different. Bob Popovics's 3D Baitfish and Capt. Gene Quigley's Geno's Baby Angel are great examples of flies that call attention and say, "Here I am . . . eat me!" Unlike poppers that probe the near-surface waters for more aggressive fish, attractor streamer patterns like these are great choices for searching deeper in the water column for fish that are a little hesitant to crash a surface fly, but may readily attack one retrieved below the surface.

Quite often while I've fished for false albacore off Jersey and North Carolina, there were fairly large numbers of baitfish present. Pods of albies would be crashing on the bait, but our epoxy-head silverside imitators would often go untouched. They were great imitations of the naturals— but that was precisely the problem. With all the natural baitfish, our imitators simply got lost in the mix. This past year was no exception. I was fishing with my friend Rick Bender, who's an exceptional and creative tier. Rick was prepared for this scenario and had tied up some epoxy-head silversides that were slightly larger then the naturals and had quite a bit more flash. It only took a cast or two before the effectiveness of Rick's creation was evident. The albies had no problem finding our offerings, and we enjoyed consistent hook-ups.

EXPERIMENTATION AND CUSTOMIZATION

It's often said that necessity is the mother of invention. As with most endeavors, experimentation and customization can, and often does, lead to innovation and a higher level of understanding of the discipline in question. This is certainly true for fly tying and fly selection for your fishing needs. You need not be a veteran of fly fishing for 20 years or more to begin experimenting with and customizing your fly patterns or those of others.

Every saltwater fly-fishing angler ought to have at least several weighted-eye/weighted-head flies in his fly box. The pattern has proven exceptional at catching fish. Now, don't get me wrong. I think weighted-eye/head flies are great; in fact I use them quite often. However, years ago I learned that making hundreds of casts in a day using weighted flies can get a bit tiring. Also, when those weighted eyes/head hit the hull of a boat occasionally, they can really do a job on the gel coat. I began experimenting to come up with a fly pattern that was easier to cast but would still have a slight dipping action on the pause during the retrieve. Of course, it would still have to be a very effective fish catcher. From this experimentation I wound up developing a streamer pattern variation that I call a "Pretender." Instead of weighted eyes, I used an enlarged epoxy head to provide enough weight to cause the fly to dip downward on the pause. The enlarged epoxy head also permitted the incorporation of large Mylar/prismatic eyes to further enhance fish attraction. The epoxy was considerably lighter than the weighted eyes, making the fly much easier to cast. But my experimentation didn't stop there. The fly's tail and wing material was primarily bucktail (chartreuse over white) that wasn't very flashy. I added a flash tail of Flashabou, a body of pearl Mylar piping, and a flash top of aqua rainbow (bluish green) Sparkle Flash to enhance the flash and provide breathability. The Pretender had excellent movement and flash qualities on the retrieve, but also had superior flash and breathability on the pause when tied flash-top style. Most importantly, the Pretender caught lots of fish. To further enhance the fly's effectiveness, small rattles can easily be tied inside the Mylar piping.

This original experimentation led to the development of an entire series of Pretender fly pattern variations that include attractor and simulator patterns for silversides, baby bunker, herring, mullet, and more. These baitfish and others can be simulated easily by simply varying the color of the bucktail and flash top and lengthening the fly with the use of saddle hackles. Pretenders have proven themselves effective time and again on species that include albies, stripers, bluefish, weakfish, Spanish macs, jack crevalle, and snook.

Experimentation and customization does not even have to be as involved as the example of the Pretender above. It can involve some simple customization that will enhance a fly pattern's effectiveness for certain situations. Take Jack Gartside's silverside Corsair imitation. Corsair generally makes a great silverside imitation all by itself. To increase the attractiveness of the fly, Jack and others inserted strands of Krystal Flash through the entire body, with the excess used as a tail. While these variations were effective, I wanted to enhance the fly further with more translucency and more flash. After playing around with different materials, I came up with a variation that I call "Silverside-In." A section of small-diameter pearl Mylar piping run through the inside of the Corsair, with the end section cut long and picked apart for a tail, gave me what I was looking for. The pearl Mylar piping gave the fly a greater illusion of translucency and closely resembled the silvery pearlescent stripe of a silverside. Silverside-Ins worked great on stripers and were especially effective for busting albies along North Carolina. When I couldn't buy a bite in Puerto Rico on finicky baby tarpon, the Silverside-In accounted for three quick takes after other flies had gone untouched.

Customization doesn't always have to wait until you get home to your fly-tying bench. You can make some simple, yet effective customizations right on the water. For instance, if you have fish refusing your bait because it appears they're looking for a shorter or thinner-profile bait, carry a pair of scissors and trim the fly a little at a time until you find the right profile. On other occasions, your fly just might not have the right color. Carry a set of Sharpie markers in assorted colors and try adding some color to entice a strike. Simply running a green marker along the top of a Clouser Floating Minnow made the difference one day for albies.

THE VITAL FEW

Selecting the right tool for the job should not be any different from selecting the right fly for the fishing situation. Just as you wouldn't expect any tool to be right for any job, you also should not expect that just any ol' fly will work for the situations you encounter. Crafting and selection of flies requires forethought and an understanding of the quarry, their preferences, prevalent baitfish in the area, conditions, and more. To be successful fly fishing in salt water, anglers need to be able to select the vital few flies from the trivial many. It's very easy for the novice saltwater fly fisher to get distracted by the sheer multitude of fly patterns that are available on

The author with a big 10-pound bonefish taken on a tan Bam-Boozle while sight fishing on the flats of Turks and Caicos Islands. The Bam-Boozle matched the tan colored bottom of the flats and proved to be deadly. Over 25 bones between 7 and 10 pounds were caught and released in a single day.

the market today. Just remember, many of these flies are designed to catch anglers . . . not fish. Many of these flies will catch some fish in some situations. Only some of these flies—the vital few—are proven fish catchers.

There is no one fly that will catch all fish in all situations. However, some informal surveys have been conducted over the years, and they seem to always indicate two preferred patterns and colors. The two fly colors identified most frequently as being the best all-around fish catchers are all-white or chartreuse over white. The two fly patterns identified most frequently as being the best all-around fish catchers should be no surprise . . . Lefty's Deceiver and Bob Clouser's Deep Minnow. This is quite understandable, since the great majority of baitfish found worldwide are generally white or silvery in appearance with a slightly darker back, and the actions that can be imparted for Deceivers and Clousers on the retrieve and pause are very baitfishlike. Needless to say, I fish with a fair amount of white-ish Deceiver-like and weighted-eye/head fly patterns in a variety of sizes.

There are two basic questions you need to answer in order to determine the flies you'll need to be successful:
1. What gamefish will I be targeting and what baits do they feed on?
2. What type of bait and what size may be available when and where I go fishing?

Once these questions are answered, you ought to be prepared with a few simulators, imitators, and attractors of the different baits and sizes you are likely to encounter. I like to put the odds in my favor as much as possible, so I generally use simulator patterns that will pass for any number of different baitfish, are fairly good imitations, and possess a good amount of flash as an attractor. Selecting flies that combine all three types increases my chances of success—and it ought to increase yours as well. The Lefty's Deceiver is a fly pattern that lends itself well to being tied in a variety of colors and sizes to simulate and even imitate a wide array of baitfish. Dan Blanton's Sar-Mul-Mac is a great example of a well-known West Coast fly pattern that combines the three types of flies while doing a good job simulating a sardine, mullet, or mackerel. One of my favorite fall patterns for the mid-Atlantic coastal area is a Pretender Bunker. While I primarily use it as a simulator for baby bunker, it really is a pretty darn good imitation of this prevalent baitfish. It's also a good simulator for other medium-sized baitfish in the area, such as herring and mullet, and a good attractor with a fair amount of flash.

Use the same strategy if you're planning to fish for bones or redfish. Select a pattern like the Gotcha or the Bam-Boozle. These are great simulators and have a fair amount of flash to attract attention. With soft, supple wing materials, they also possess high breathability and will usually get the go-ahead when examined up close by a bone. Just vary the color of the fly to match the different-colored bottoms you might encounter.

What's especially important is selecting several go-to flies that you can fish with confidence. I can't quite explain it, but many anglers don't seem to fish a fly with the same level of enthusiasm when they don't believe it will be effective. This usually translates to reduced action, ineffectiveness, and . . . no fish. Fishing with a few flies that are handpicked for the occasion based on experience can have a positive influence on an angler's confidence and his success. Select the vital few that will work for you.

STRATEGY 4—USE THE RIGHT FLY

Just as no one tool is right for all jobs, no one fly is right for all fishing situations. And just as a carpenter would carry an assortment of select tools around his waist for the variety of jobs that he may encounter, so too should a saltwater fly-fishing angler carry a select variety of different flies.

- Characteristics of flies: Profile.
    Color.
    Buoyancy.
    Breathability.
    Translucency.
- Three types of flies: Simulators.
    Imitators.
    Attractors.
- Experiment and customize.
- Select the vital few.

MAXIMIZE YOUR PRESENTATION

Being in the right place at the right time with the right fly is still no guarantee that you will catch fish. Anglers who are routinely success-ful have learned to maximize their presentation. You'll need to do the same if you wish to be successful too. Sure, there are times when fly fishing the salt is like child's play. Sometimes it doesn't seem to matter what fly you have tied on the end of your line or how your fly is presented . . . the fish just seem to throw themselves on it. Yes, there are times like these, but by and large these are exceptions to the rule rather than the norm. Take advantage of these times, because as you spend more time on the water, you will learn that there will be many tough times ahead when your skills in maximizing your presentation will be critical to your success. Here are some tactics for maximizing your presentations.

FLY LINES

A fly line's primary purpose is to carry the fly in the air to the target. That's the simplified version. However, there's more to it than that. There is a multitude of different fly lines available today to handle a wide variety of different fishing scenarios and angler casting preferences. It's important to point out that you should learn and become proficient in casting a weight-forward floating or intermediate fly line first before you attempt to cast the wide assortment of weighted lines and shooting-head systems.

Look at fly lines as tools to perform a particular job. Just as there are different tools for different jobs, so too are there different fly lines for different fly-fishing scenarios. In salt water, one fly line will not be well suited for

Nonwilting floating fly lines and long tapered leaders are essential for fishing skinny waters of the Tropics for species like bonefish, permit, and this redfish from the back bays of Sanibel Island in southwest Florida.

all situations. For the great majority of saltwater fishing situations where a floating or intermediate fly line is desirable, you ought to use a weight-forward line. The reason for this is that you'll need to be able to load your rod with a minimal number of false casts (three or less) to deliver the fly quickly and minimize fatigue. Weight-forward floating and intermediate lines come in a variety of weight-forward tapers. For short to medium casts, a saltwater taper having a line with a shorter front taper, belly, and rear taper will have more weight concentrated in the forward part of the line. This is highly desirable for short, quick casts. This type of taper will also benefit novice and intermediate saltwater fly casters, as it will make loading the rod easier. More experienced anglers who are routinely casting longer distances and thus having to carry more line in the air will generally find a conventional weight forward more desirable. The reason for this is that conventional weight-forward lines spread the weight out over a longer distance by having a longer front taper, belly, and back taper. Of course, today there are almost as many different weight-forward tapers as there are anglers. The taper you select should be based upon your casting ability, style, and the fishing scenarios you're likely to encounter.

Another important consideration is selecting a fly line (floating or intermediate) that has the desired stiffness or suppleness to match the climates you'll be fishing. Years ago, before the development of all the new fly lines we have today, I was fishing southwest Florida in the Ten Thousand Islands for snook and redfish. We were sight fishing, so we spent a fair amount of time on the bow of the boat in the ready position. It was summer, and it was hot. About 20 minutes went by without spotting a fish when suddenly we had a pair of nice reds cruising about 70 feet out. I went to load the rod and found that the line, which had been lying on the deck, was tacky and as limp as a wet noodle. Try as I might, I could not get the line to slip smoothly through the guides or my fingers. By the time I got enough line out to load the rod and make the cast, the fish were long gone. The fly line in those days just was not made to handle the extreme temperatures encountered in the Tropics during the course of a day.

Where there is a need, there is innovation. Several years later a few companies began to market fly lines specifically designed for use under the hot tropical sun that wouldn't wilt. These new lines are wonderful. What a difference! Soon after, fly-line manufacturers also realized that while these lines and others with mono or braided mono cores cast beautifully in warm weather, they performed miserably in colder weather along the mid- and northern Atlantic regions. While the early mono and braided mono core lines provided much-needed stiffness for tropical fishing, they retained too much stiffness in colder climates and caused excessive coil memory; tangles and inefficient casting resulted.

Today it's a different story. Line manufacturers now offer a wide range of fly lines that are designed specifically for areas of different temperatures. What a welcome relief! When selecting a fly line, be sure to read the manufacturer's information on that particular line. Check to see that you have the right taper for your fishing preferences and whether it is suitable for tropical, temperate, or colder climates.

Additional advancements in fly-line design include the new slick finishes and thinner running lines. These two advancements have really increased the castability of these lines. Not only will you find that they are easier and more enjoyable to cast and shoot, but you will also find that they will add yards to your casting distance.

There is, however, another important purpose of modern fly lines—to carry the fly to the target under the water. That's right! With the advent of modern sinking lines and shooting heads, fly anglers are no longer limited to just fishing the upper few feet of the water column. We can now effectively fish water from the surface to depths over 20 feet and put the fly right where the fish are. As I mentioned in strategy 4, the weight of the fly line, not the fly, should be used to carry the fly to the desired depth of the fish.

One summer a few years back, I was striper fishing the outflow of a power plant in the middle Chesapeake. I was quite familiar with the drill for this location and was fishing a Teeny 450-grain weighted line to get the fly down about 10 or 15 feet to where the fish were holding. It has a sink rate of approximately 8 inches per second. I was hooking up on a regular basis. These were not big fish, but they were keeping my 8-weight bent so I was happy. During this time I had noticed a fellow fly rodder fishing about 200 yards farther out in the flow who wasn't having any luck. Even from a quarter mile I could see the reason why . . . he was using a floating line and wasn't getting the fly down to the fish. About an hour passed by when I noticed that the other angler was idling his boat up in my vicinity to check out the action. He approached the area I was fishing very quietly. This really showed respect for my fishing. I returned the favor by waving him to get closer and position his boat close to mine so he might share the bounty. He proceeded to fish for about 15 minutes without any success. I didn't know how receptive he would be to some suggestions, but I figured after seeing me catch and release four or five fish during this time, it was a safe bet that he might be willing to try something different. I called over to him and found that he did have a 400-grain weighted line. I suggested that he use the weighted line and let it sink for about 20 seconds (about 13 feet) while feeding slack line before beginning his retrieve. On his second cast he came tight to a feisty schoolie bass. Needless to say, he was very happy. Over the next two hours, he was hooking up with consistency and caught and released quite a few bass. It was a magical time for him, and I was happy to have been a part of it. A few hours later after I had just pulled my boat out, the other angler caught up to me, introduced himself, and thanked me for the help I gave him. He mentioned that he had tried saltwater fly fishing a number of times before without much success. That day, he said, was the best day he'd ever had. He was absolutely thrilled and thanked me again. That was my magical moment. It made my three-hour ride home a pleasant one. What a difference a line can make!

Floating Lines

Floating lines are the lines most anglers are familiar with, since they are used for most freshwater fishing situations. Floating lines can be used not only for fishing shallow water, but also to fish the surface and upper 3 feet of the water column effectively. If fish can be seen busting bait or finning on the surface, a floating line would be a good choice to get your fly into the strike zone. A floating line will also provide the best opportunity to quickly pick the line off the water to deliver another cast. With a little practice, you should be able to easily pick 40 feet of line off the water. This is especially important when sight fishing in shallow waters for bonefish, redfish, snook, tarpon, permit, or stripers. It can also be important when you're in deep water and fish like stripers, blues, Spanish mackerel, false albacore, bonito, and jacks are feeding at the surface. The ability to quickly pick up your fly line off the surface without having to retrieve it all the way back and make repeated casts will greatly enhance your hook-ups.

Floating lines are also very effective when surf fishing in the wash or off jetties, and when fishing tidal rips that have structure several feet below the surface. A floating line can keep your fly in the strike zone without hanging up on the bottom or in the structure below. Fishing floating lines in open water for fish feeding on or near the surface may be a disadvantage in some situations in that you will be restricted to effectively fishing only about the top 3 feet of water. While on some occasions you may see an awful lot of fish busting on the surface, you can bet that about 10 times as many fish are below the surface. In these situations, a floating line will not be efficient in reaching the bulk of fish feeding farther down in the water column. This may require that you change rods or spools or, worse yet, have to put on another line. In either case, you would be missing out on valuable fishing time. An alternative would be to use an intermediate fly line.

Intermediate Fly Lines

In recent years intermediate weight-forward (WF) fly lines have become enormously popular because of their versatility in being able to effectively fish the top 4 or 5 feet of the water column as well as the surface. Being able to fish poppers, sliders, and subsurface flies all with the same fly line gives anglers greater versatility. With an average sink rate of 1½ to 2½ inches per second, intermediate lines can deliver your fly right smack in front of the fish you're pursuing. Casting and beginning your retrieve right away will keep your fly tracking up near the surface. Pausing after casting or during the retrieve will allow the fly line to sink a bit more to get the fly in the strike zone.

When fishing deeper water, I usually have one reel spool or rod set up with a sinking line and the other with an intermediate. When fish such as stripers, trout, blues, Spanish macs, and albies are working bait near the surface, I can effectively fish a popper or slider on the surface, or go a few feet below if that happens to be their feeding preference. The important thing is that I don't have to worry about losing valuable fishing time changing lines. Another benefit of using intermediate lines when fishing for tarpon and permit is that an intermediate line will sink just below the surface and cause any eelgrass or other debris to slip off and therefore prevent any hang-ups on the line that could alarm a fish.

Clear Fly Lines

Another important development in the last few years is clear-tip or full-clear floating and intermediate fly lines. Clear fly lines enable an angler to essentially lengthen his leader. In my experience, this is a major advantage in favor of the angler when fishing near the surface in clear waters and when fishing for wary fish, especially if they see quite a bit of pressure.

Clear fly lines are excellent choices when fishing for albies, stripers, sea trout, and the like in clear waters. However, full-clear fly lines will be somewhat of a disadvantage when sight fishing for species such as tarpon, bonefish, and permit when it is critical that you know where your fly is at all times. If you lose sight of your fly with a colored floating fly line, you can quickly track your line with your eye to locate your fly. If you're using a clear line, you won't be able to. Fly-line color is far less significant when fishing sinking lines, particularly when fishing waters with low visibility. False albacore, for example, have excellent eyesight. When fishing near the surface in clear waters, clear fly lines will definitely increase your hook-ups. Yet when you're fishing deeper in the water column with sinking lines that have a dark forward weighted section, albies and other species don't appear to be turned off by the line color. This makes perfect sense since light and, therefore, visibility are greatly reduced as the depth is increased.

Sinking Lines/Shooting Heads

The development of sinking lines and shooting heads has really increased the volume of water that can be effectively fished with a fly. Previously, saltwater anglers were only able to search the near-surface waters with their flies. Now with heavily weighted lines and shooting heads that have sink rates ranging from 2 to almost 12 inches per second, you can get your line down to the depths to search for your elusive quarry. Sinking lines are continuous lines with a seamless connection of the forward sinking portion of the line—which can vary from 24 to 30 inches or more—to the balance of the rear portion of the line, which is typically a level floating fly line of a thinner/lighter diameter. Sinking shooting heads, on the other hand, are just the forward sinking/weighted portion of the line that is attached to a lighter running line of thinner diameter (usually braided mono) via a loop-to-loop connection, which is then attached to the backing.

When fishing along beaches, inlets, and back bays, I prefer using a shooting-head system. The major advantage of using the shooting-head system when on foot is that you only need to take one rod and reel and can quickly change shooting heads with loop-to-loop connections for different fishing situations. With a shooting-head system, you can easily carry four or five different shooting heads in small lightweight coils. For example, a complement of floating, intermediate, 200-grain, and 400-grain shooting heads would cover you from the surface down to over 15 feet. Shooting heads can be purchased from a number of different suppliers, or you can make your own with lead core line and braided mono as a running line. Sinking shooting heads made from lead core line can be beneficial to anglers in cutting costs but also because lead core line is of a thinner diameter, so it has a slightly faster sink rate. When fishing from a boat, I mostly prefer using sinking lines that use level floating fly line as the running line. The fly line is much easier on the hands as opposed to the more abrasive braided mono running line. A boat also has room to store additional rods and reels already loaded with different lines.

I think it's important to point out that the primary purpose of sinking lines/shooting heads is not just to get the fly to sink, but also to get the fly down into the strike zone reasonably fast. When fishing the depths, time is fish! By this I mean that the longer you have to wait for your fly line to reach the optimum strike-zone depth, the less time you'll have to catch fish. Conversely, the faster your fly reaches the strike zone, the more fish you'll potentially catch. (See the illustration "Getting Down into the Strike Zone"). Unfortunately, one sinking line or shooting head will not be the best line for all fishing situations. This is simply because these lines are designed to sink at different rates, and the fish you are pursuing will be located at different depths at different times.

For anglers new to the salt and sinking lines/shooting heads, I recommend fishing only with a line/head that you are comfortable with and proficient in casting. Usually this means casting with sinking lines/shooting heads from about 200 to about 350 grains. If matched to 7- to 9-weight rods, even a novice should easily handle these lines. This, of course, is providing the correct method of casting weighted lines is used as described for strategy 2. While these light to midrange lines may not be the optimum sinking line/head for getting down to deeper-holding fish, they will enable you to cast proficiently without being frustrated and having problems. You just might need to wait a little longer for your line to reach the strike zone. As you become more accustomed to casting sinking lines/shooting heads, you can begin casting heavier lines when the situation calls for it. Another important point to remember is that in most situations it's not desirable to cast long distances from a boat when you're trying to reach fish that are holding in deeper water of 15 feet or more. A short cast of 30 to 40 feet is all that is needed since you'll need to manually feed slack line out the rod tip to maintain a drag-free drift, which will allow the line and fly to sink freely without drag. You may need to feed out 60 to 80 feet or more of fly line and some backing to reach the desired depth. This coupled with a 30- to 40-foot cast will put the fly at distance of between 90 and 120 feet.

As often is the case, many of the wonderful folks who book fishing trips are not proficient casters, and many never fish sinking lines. Such was the case a few years ago. A gentleman had booked a fishing trip in December to fish off the Jersey coast and try his luck at striped bass. When anglers are not proficient fly casters, I always hope for large pods of breaking fish or at least fish that are holding in deeper water where a long cast usually isn't critical. We had no luck fishing the morning along the edges of jetties and had not spotted any fish working the surface. After lunch I spotted a few birds working a line about 5 miles offshore and found some fish holding about 15 or 20 feet down. My client found casting the 450-grain weighted line awkward and could only manage about a 40-foot cast. This certainly wasn't anything to be ashamed about, since he'd only had his first fly-casting lesson a few hours before.

Believe it or not, bluefish can get pretty fussy. With light wire leaders getting refused, Greg Mentzer switched to a mono leader. He was cut off a few times, but he managed to stay connected and land several nice bluefish like this one.

Based upon his experience level, he was doing quite well and was up for the challenge. Enthusiasm goes a long way. I assured him that the distance was perfect for catching these fish. He made his cast in great shape and proceeded to feed out slack line. I instructed him to shake out and feed slack line while he counted down for about 35 seconds before beginning his retrieve. Maintaining slack line is essential for allowing the line to sink freely. To determine out how much time you need to allow for sinking, just convert the depth the fish are holding at to inches (20 x 12 = 240 inches). Then divide that number by the sink rate (450 grains = 8 inches per second) of the sinking line you're using (240÷8 = 30 seconds). After 30 seconds his fly was at least 20 feet down and in excellent position for a strike. He started his retrieve and after only a few strips he was tight to his first striper—by the way, a respectable 10 pounds. What a great magical moment for my guest, and for me being there to share it with him. After that first fish, he was a true believer in sinking lines. Amazingly, with a bit of confidence, his casting improved with each fish.

Since sinking fly lines are substantially heavier (more mass), they will enable you to cast much larger flies with the same effort. This is an important consideration when fishing for species such as stripers or bluefish that may be feeding on large 10- to 12-inch bunker. A well-known fact is that to consistently catch large stripers, you'll need to use large flies. Smaller flies will just be ignored.

LEADERS

Leaders are a critical component necessary for maximizing your presentations. They have a number of important functions, including:
- Keeping your fly line connected to your fly/fish.
- Providing an "invisible" connection to your fly line.
- Turning your fly over.
- Providing distance between your fly and fly line.
- Imparting the right action to the fly.
- Keeping your fly tracking at the same depth as your fly line.

Keeping your fly line connected to your fly/fish is obviously a critical function of a leader. For trout-fishing situations, a tapered leader is used, which progressively gets smaller in diameter as it gets closer to the fly or the end of the leader. Tapered leaders are also used for many species of saltwater fish, including redfish, permit, and bonefish, which have soft mouths. However, this is not the case for saltwater fish with sharp teeth or abrasive mouths such as bluefish, mackerel, 'cuda, tarpon, and snook. For these fish you will need a shock tippet of heavy mono or metal leader. A shock tippet is a short, heavier piece of mono generally 12 to 18 inches in length that is tied to your fly and the end of your weight-class tippet. If you're trying for a world record, remember that the total length of your shock tippet cannot exceed 12 inches, including the knots. A shock tippet can vary widely from 20-50 pounds for baby tarpon, snook, stripers, and even small blues and Spanish macs to as much as 60 to 100 pounds for large tarpon and billfish. A short (6- to 12-inch) piece of wire ranging from 15 to 30 pounds is recommended for fish with serious dentures. Keep in mind that in many situations, the number of strikes may decrease as you increase the diameter of the shock tippet. Seek to find the right balance where you will get enough fish to take your fly while being able to stay connected to land the fish. Sometimes you may need to land fewer fish in order to get hooked up. Only use heavy shock tippets and especially wire where and when you need to do so. Just remember . . . if you can't get it to take your fly, you won't have any shot at catching a fish. Better to lose a few and catch some. Stripers, for example, are wire-shy and usually will not strike a fly tied to a heavy tippet or wire leader. Wire leaders are also not necessary or recommended for other species like gray/speckled trout and false albacore that have pointy teeth for gripping but that rarely, if ever, cut even light mono.

When constructing leaders, it's important to always have a section of the leader that is below the tested weight of your backing. If a large, fast fish like a bone, permit, tarpon, or tuna is screaming off your backing, it's better to break the fish off by turning down the drag or adding hand pressure than risk losing everything including your fly line. This is also an important consideration if you are fishing with sinking lines that can get fouled on bottom structure. For example, if you have 30-pound backing, make sure your tippet is less than 30-pound test. In most saltwater fishing scenarios you'll be using tippets of 20-pound test or less and will not have a problem. If you need to use a heavier shock tippet—40 pounds or more— you'll need to ensure that a class tippet of less than 30-pound test is tied between the shock tippet and the end of your leader.

Another key function of leaders is *providing an "invisible" connection to your fly line* . . . well, almost invisible. Actually, monofilament leaders are somewhat translucent and can be seen in clear water. However, in many saltwater fishing environments the water is often off-color, stained, or otherwise turbid to some degree—which camouflages the leader's presence. We are also fortunate that most saltwater species usually aren't leader-shy. Most saltwater fish have never seen a leader and have never been hooked. There are exceptions, however. Species with excellent eyesight in very clear and/or shallow water such as false albacore, bonefish, permit, and sometimes even stripers will often refuse leader tippets tied with regular monofilament. At the very least you'll have far fewer hook-ups unless you use fluorocarbon for your tippets. When chumming albies close by the boat (within 10 feet), I have observed them reject a fly tied on regular mono. After putting on a fluorocarbon tippet of the same pound test and tying on the same exact fly, albie after albie would take the fly without hesitation. Big dumb bonefish found where there is minimal fishing pressure usually aren't very leader-shy. However, if you are going to fish for bones in Florida or other locations where there is much higher fishing pressure, I strongly recommend using fluorocarbon for your tippet. These fish see a lot of flies and are exceptionally wary. Anything that looks the slightest bit unusual will be refused. Yes, fluorocarbon is more expensive, but our fishing time is precious . . . catching time is priceless. My advice is to take no chances; if there is even the slightest likelihood of fish being cautious of a mono tippet, use fluorocarbon.

The importance of *turning your fly over* is sometimes an overlooked essential for proper presentation. Any ol' leader could be placing your fly and leader in a heap at the end of your casts. The key is to use leaders that have a thicker butt section of 30- to 50-pound test that extends about half the length of the total leader, with the remainder of the leader tied with progressively thinner mono. This is important in transferring the energy from the fly line all the way to the end of the leader so that it will unroll correctly and turn the fly over for a smooth presentation. For this reason, avoid using stiff mono for the butt section. With the exception of flats fishing on dead-calm days, the great majority of saltwater fly fishing requires only midlength to fairly short leaders of 4 to 8 feet. Keeping your leader as short as necessary for your fishing situation will help make casting easier while avoiding problems. Saltwater neophytes are often trout fishermen as well and make the mistake of continuing to use exceptionally long leaders when they are unnecessary. Keep it simple by keeping your leaders only as long as the conditions require.

Even when casting smaller saltwater flies to bones, redfish, stripers, or albies, a properly constructed leader is essential for getting a fish to take your fly. For flats-type fishing, longer leaders of 10 to 12 feet with light 8- to 12-pound tippets are typically required for an effective presentation that won't alarm the fish. Leaders of 14 to 16 feet may be required for spooky fish in very shallow water on flat-calm days. A key characteristic of any good leader is that it starts off thicker at the butt section, which is tied/looped to the end of the fly line, and progressively gets thinner toward the end that's attached to the fly. You can purchase ready-made knotless leaders, but they may not always be the length you need. Even if you buy your leaders, you ought to know how to construct them if needed. Additionally, it should also be noted that larger, heavier, and more air-resistant flies require heavier leaders to turn them over.

The best formula for constructing long leaders (10 to 16 feet) is the well-known formula used by Lefty Kreh and one that I also have found to be very effective over the years. Start by using the same brand of mono throughout, with the exception possibly of using fluorocarbon for your class tippet. Use a premium spinning line from any reputable manufacturer. This line will be flexible enough to unroll smoothly when casting.

LEFTY'S LEADER FORMULA

For 9-weight outfits and heavier, use 50-pound-test mono for the butt section. For outfits of 8-weight or less, use 40-pound test. If, for example, you are tying a 10-foot leader to be used on a 9-weight outfit, start with 5 feet of 50-pound mono or half the length of the leader. To the butt section tie 18 inches of 40-pound followed by 1 foot of 30-pound and 1 foot of 20-pound. Lastly, tie on 18 inches of your class tippet and you're done. For longer leaders, lengthen each strand accordingly.

Providing distance between your fly and fly line can be an important consideration. When casting smaller flies in shallow water on flat-calm days, it is usually the slap of the fly line that alerts the fish to your presence. While 12-foot leaders may be the norm for most flats-fishing scenarios, calm conditions and spooky fish may warrant 14- or even 16-foot leaders. However, as I mentioned above, most typical saltwater fly-fishing situations only require leaders of 4 to 8 feet in length. When fishing sinking lines, I usually only use a 4-foot leader. I typically use 2 feet of 30-pound mono for the butt section with a double surgeon's loop at each end. To this

I do a loop-to-loop connection with 2 feet of mono ranging anywhere from 12 to 20 pounds. This is a very simple, yet effective leader for most of the saltwater fly fishing that I do along the Atlantic coast. It's easy to tie on the water and very inexpensive. Some excellent anglers just use a straight piece of 20-pound mono for many of their leaders. Fly fishing does not have to be complicated. Keep it simple.

Leaders and, more specifically, tippets play a key function in *imparting the right action to the fly.* For flies to be effective, they need to simulate life-like actions. This cannot be done when the tippet is too heavy and thick. The fly will have little natural movement and will be simply dragged along like a piece of wood. As a general rule, the smaller the hook size, the lighter the tippet; conversely, the larger the hook size, the heavier the tippet. Flies on hook sizes 8 to 4 will perform well when tied to a tippet ranging from 6- to 10-pound test. Hook sizes 4 to 1 will perform well on tippets from 10- to 15-pound test, and 1 to 4/0 hooks on tippets from 12- to 30-pound test. When fishing for snook and baby tarpon, heavier shock tippets in the 20- to 40-pound range are required because of their extremely abrasive mouths. Shock tippets ranging from 40- to 100-pound test are required for large tarpon. Tie the fly to your tippet using a Homer Rhode loop knot to impart action to the fly even when using these heavier/thicker tippets.

Keeping your fly tracking at the same depth as your fly line is essential when fishing in deeper water with sinking lines. One of the most significant mistakes that I see novice saltwater fly fishermen make routinely when fishing deep water is using leaders that are too long. Saltwater fish are generally not leader-shy. They are even less leader-shy the deeper you go. Monofilament leaders are more buoyant than the weighted sinking tips, hence they will not sink at the same rate. A long leader will therefore cause your fly to have a tendency to ride slightly higher in the water column than your weighted fly line. Two problems result: First, your fly will not be tracking as deep as your fly line—which may mean your fly is not in the strike zone—and second, slack is developed between your fly and the fly line, which means you may miss strikes. In both situations, long leaders fished deep usually translates to anglers missing out on more hook-up opportunities. To increase your odds of success, keep things simple . . . shorten your leader. When fishing the water column below 4 feet, only use leaders from 3 to 5 feet in length—you'll notice a huge difference. If you are fishing with floating or intermediate lines and want to keep your fly down with longer leaders, try using complete fluorocarbon leaders. Fluoro-carbon is denser than mono and will sink with the fly.

APPROACHING YOUR QUARRY

Any good trout fisherman will tell you that a surefire way to reduce your opportunities for catching fish is to alert the fish to your presence. The same is true for saltwater fly fishing. Yes, saltwater species are generally much tougher and more ferocious. Yes, they do not seem to spook easily, especially when feeding in large schools. And yes, you may still catch a lot of fish without being careful. But by and large, if you learn to approach fish quietly without alerting them, you will discover that you not only catch more fish, but also catch more big fish.

By Boat

Most shallow-water anglers understand the importance of stealth whether wade fishing or fishing from a boat. However, many boating anglers must either be unaware or ignore the importance of stealth when fishing deeper water along the mid- and northern Atlantic coast.

Greg Mentzer hooked up to a false albacore. When bait is scarce, albies will often fol-low shrimp trawlers to feed on the by-catch. A good captain, a well-positioned boat, and . . . voilà! (Photo: Greg and Carol Mentzer)

DRIFT FISHING OVER SUBSURFACE FISH

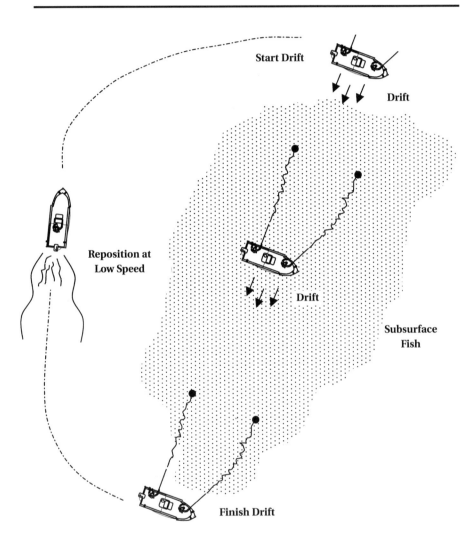

After locating subsurface fish, take note of their depth on the fish finder and shut down the engine to begin your drift. Select a sinking line that will deliver your fly into the strike zone quickly. Fish will face into the oncoming current to feed, so you will need to make quartering or downcurrent casts. This will put your fly in front of the fish and make it easier to maintain a tight line to detect strikes. Once hooked up, take note of the depth and mark your location on the GPS. After drifting past the fish, reposition the boat for another drift by circling out and around the school so as not to spook or alarm the fish.

It was late December, and my close friend Greg Mentzer and I were fishing for stripers just off Long Beach Island and Seaside Park, New Jersey from my 18-foot center console. When we were heading north out of Barnegat Inlet, things looked promising. There were hundreds of birds working an area about 2 or 3 miles offshore.

Unfortunately, there were also quite a large number of boats in the area. We cruised the outside edges of the fleet, hoping to mark fish on the fish finder, but no such luck. No one was hooking up in the other boats. There was plenty of bait in the area, so there had to be stripers too. I've seen this scenario way too often. I surmised that stripers were probably working the school throughout the night and into the early-morning hours until the fleet of boats arrived on the scene, when they probably began to run over and through them. Contrary to popular belief, stripers—like most fish—do not like boat noise and traffic and will leave the area, scatter, and/or go down to deeper water to get relief. Fishing continues, but catching really suffers.

Finding this to be the case, we headed the boat away from the fleet and searched for our own fish in quieter waters. We were drifting between the fleet and shore, searching the waters with sinking lines and large attractor streamers. I routinely scanned nearby waters with my binoculars in case some action picked up just out of eyesight range. Scanning toward shore, I saw a group of surf casters working an area of beach and noticed a few birds working the water about half a mile off the beach. The bird activity stopped after a few minutes. After a short while I scanned the same area and noticed a few birds working the same area again. I ran the boat over, cut back the motor so our approach would be quiet, and idled in closer for a look-see. The wind was blowing hard out of the west, and as we drifted into 20-foot water the fish finder began chirping and marking stripers along the bottom. I turned the engine over and idled the boat about 100 yards closer to shore to begin our drift. We were both fishing 550-grain weighted lines, and when we hit the 20-foot depth Greg hooked up. A short while later my line came tight also. After drifting over the holding stripers, I quietly repositioned the boat for another drift by circling back to avoid running over the fish we were drifting over. We repeated this routine for approximately two hours and consistently hooked several stripers during each drift, including a 40-incher. Our faces were beet red from the cold wind, but we didn't care . . . we were catching fish!

During this two-hour period the terns would continue to work the water in the area we were fishing for a short while, and then they would stop. No other boats came within half a mile of our location. That is, not until the birds continued working over the water for a much longer period. I could see the fish coming closer to the surface on the depthfinder. The stripers were working the bait closer to the surface, and the birds knew it and didn't call off their attack. Unfortunately for Greg and me, the increased and prolonged bird activity caught the attention of a few boats. Within just minutes we had about 10 boats charge the area of bird activity with motors blazing. They'd stop abruptly and begin chucking jigs and casting flies in the hope of hooking up. A few other boats were trying to catch fish by trolling back and forth, through and around us. Not one of them caught a single fish, but neither did we. Because these other boats went fishless, they were convinced there weren't any fish there to be caught. Within just about 10 minutes of bursting on the scene, the boats were gone. We held tight and continued our routine. I was still marking the same pod of fish, but they now had lockjaw. They were spooked from all the boat noise and hunkered down to wait until it got quiet again. It did, and after about 30 minutes we were again catching stripers. Our success in this scenario was due to our ability to locate fish and keep the noise level down to a minimum. I believe this is an excellent example of how some anglers may locate fish, but alert or otherwise spook the fish to the point that they either leave the area or develop lockjaw. This can happen from a boat or when wade fishing if you're not careful.

Anglers fly fishing the flats or shallow waters of 6 feet or less, and especially those who sight fish, appear to learn very quickly that boat noise will decrease the odds of success. Sound travels a lot faster through water than air. Whether it's the loud noise from the motor or the more subtle noise from hull slap, poling, a dropped reel or hatch cover, or even loud conversation, noise ought to be minimized so to maximize your success. Competent flats guides will run fast to a promising flat, but will cut the engine a good distance out and pole quietly for 100 yards or more to get into position so as not to alert or spook any fish. The shallower and calmer the water, the more important it is to be quiet and approach in stealth mode. This applies to bone-, permit, tarpon, snook, and redfishing, as well as to other species such as stripers and even bluefish. A few years back I was fishing a flat on the upper Chesapeake Bay. Large numbers of stripers had moved up on the flats in 1 to 3 feet of water. We began catching nice fish in the 6- to 15-pound range. However, the action abruptly stopped when my client hopped off the slightly elevated bow deck. With a thump, the water boiled everywhere within 100 feet around the boat . . . game over!

There are a number of things to consider when approaching a shallow flat from a boat that you plan to pole or drift over while sight fishing in calm conditions. First, if there is a current in the area, you'll need to approach from upcurrent. Bonefish and other flats species will typically swim and feed with their noses into the oncoming current to sniff out any possible meals. The best cast is to fish approaching dead-on to the bow or slightly off either side of the boat. Second, you'll need to have the sun at your back if you're sight fishing so you can peer through the water to see your quarry; otherwise it's nearly impossible to see them with glare from the sun. If you have a potentially good location along a mangrove edge but the sun is rising behind them, creating glare, you may be able to use an alternate method. In this scenario, simply pole out along the edge of the mangroves. The mangroves will cast a fairly long shadow out from the bank, eliminating sun glare and allowing both angler and guide to search under the water. This technique may not afford the best casting angle off the side of the boat, but it may be the only angle available to spot fish that are not tailing or pushing water.

Once you've considered current and glare, you can then determine the line you'll take and plan your approach accordingly. Cut your engine to a slow idle at least 200 yards out. Then use your trolling motor or pole for the last 100 yards or so. During this final approach and as you pole or drift along the flat, you ought to scan the water ahead for signs of fish working on or near the surface. Once in position, continue to look for surface clues as well as peering through the water to spot fish under the surface. This stealth approach gives you a major advantage in that the fish are unaware of your presence and are more likely to behave naturally, giving you signs of their location. This is a common approach used for sight fishing flats and one that has proven highly effective. Anglers who have been fortunate enough to experience this type of hunting/fishing know and value the stealth approach and are more likely to apply this approach for other species such as stripers, blues, and weakfish/sea trout that can also be found on flats, but in more northern latitudes of the mid- and northern Atlantic coastal regions.

For boat anglers fishing deeper water, I still highly recommend employing stealth when approaching an area you plan to fish. For some reason, this technique is not used by most boat anglers. They usually just run in a straight line to where they will begin their drift, running right over the very fish they want to catch. This practice is self-defeating. The game may be over before you even get started. I have heard a number of boat anglers justify using this technique by stating that they still catch fish. In situations involving schooling fish like stripers, I agree—you may still catch fish, but I bet you won't catch big fish with any consistency.

When approaching schooling fish, riplines, or structure like bridges and jetties, idle down your motor at least 100 yards away and approach the area quietly. If there's current or some wind available that can assist you, take full advantage and let the wind and/or current carry or blow you right into the area you will be fishing. Hopefully, your efforts in being quiet will be rewarded with a few hook-ups. After you have drifted through and well beyond the area, restart your motor at the lowest idle possible to keep noise down. Now instead of idling back in a straight line to restart your drift, chart a crescent-shaped course, looping out away and back to your starting point, and repeat the process. Each location and situation will be slightly different. Schooling fish that are crashing bait at the surface are feeding aggressively and will usually tolerate more boat noise because of all the commotion they're causing. In these situations it may be quite acceptable to loop back to start another drift by running the boat a little faster. Try to avoid running and gunning. It's very disruptive to the fish and it could get dangerous if other boats are in the area. The behavior of the fish will tell you what's acceptable. Trust me . . . if you use this quiet approach and don't alert the fish to your presence, you will not only catch more fish but also discover that you're catching larger fish.

Keep in mind that when approaching an area, it's important to consider the impact you'll have on any other anglers in the area, whether they are fishing from other boats or from shore. Blowing up on or running close by a quiet area with motors blazing is downright rude and disrespectful to the other anglers—but I see it happen all the time. If those anglers are into fish, the last thing they want is some yahoo to put the fish down and ruin the fishing for everyone. Before rushing in with guns blazing, slow down and even shut your motor down a quarter to a half mile away to check out the situation. The easiest and quietest way to do this is by simply using a pair of binoculars. Even from that distance you should be able to clearly see the positioning and drift of other boats, any surface-feeding action, or the tell-

DRIFT FISHING FOR SURFACE-FEEDING FISH

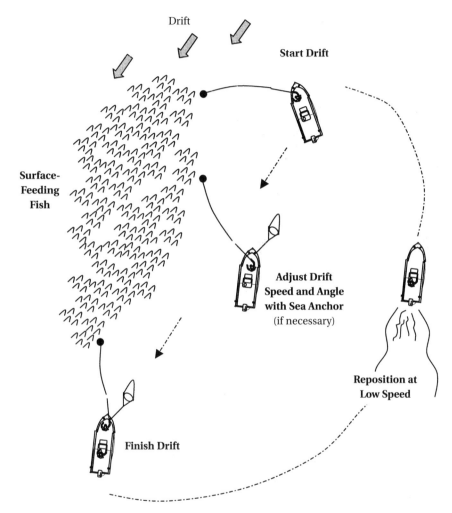

Drift

Start Drift

Surface-
Feeding
Fish

Adjust Drift
Speed and Angle
with Sea Anchor
(if necessary)

Reposition at
Low Speed

Finish Drift

Once you have located a pod or school of fish at or near the surface, idle down and position your boat upcurrent and to the side of the activity to avoid alarming or putting the fish down. As the boat drifts into the fish, cast to the edges of the activity. Floating or intermediate lines will work effectively at and near the surface. However, the use of sinking lines for species along the north and mid-Atlantic coast may yield larger striped bass or sea trout that are holding deeper. After drifting through the activity, reposition your boat by circling out and around the activity to avoid putting the fish down.

tale sign of a bent rod indicating a hooked fish. Based upon the information you obtain, you can decide on whether you want to fish the area and if so, what the best approach will be.

If there are anchored boats fishing the area, keep your distance and approach quietly. On the other hand, if other boats are drifting, you should consider their line of drift before approaching the area. Generally, you'll want to position your boat on the upcurrent/upwind side of the other boat's drift, being very careful not cross their drift line on the downcurrent/downwind side. Why, you may ask? For the same reason that we discussed earlier: If you cross over someone else's line of drift, you will be running over the fish that the other anglers are hoping to catch. This is very discourteous. If other anglers are fishing an area before you, they deserve first rights. Cutting in on someone else's action is fairly easy to avoid when there are few boats in the area. However, when the action gets fast and furious in a confined area, it can sometimes be difficult to discern who's drifting where and who's got first rights.

I was actually guilty of this infraction a few years back when fishing Beaufort Inlet in the fall during a false albacore melee. Unfortunately, my friend Rick Bender and I got caught up in some chaotic fishing during an early-morning blitz and I unintentionally crossed another guide's drift. I wasn't even aware of it until he pulled alongside and politely told me what I did and asked that I not do it again. Many anglers would have just shouted some obscenities and flipped me the bird, but he didn't. A little taken aback, but totally appreciating his politeness and concern for getting his clients some fish, I simply said I was very sorry, didn't realize what I had done, and would try not to do it again. Still not sure of what I had done, I asked Rick his opinion of the situation so I would be sure not to repeat it. Rick, the gentleman and loyal fishing partner that he is, said, "Yup . . . you f'd up!" And that was the end of that. My personal preference is to avoid close-quarter situations like this if at all possible, but if you can't, then do it safely, demonstrate common courtesy, and try to be tolerant of other anglers. You never know—you might be the one making the mistake.

Rather than continuously drifting along riplines or structure such as riprap, jetties, or bridges, consider anchoring to reduce noise and maximize your fishing. There are a number of locations that I fish several times a year along structures that I know usually hold fish. When I fish these spots, I want to minimize the noise so I maximize my opportunities to catch fish. I will approach these areas quietly as described above and make a drift or two to see if anyone's home. If I hook up, I'll usually anchor up in a position that will afford me the greatest casting window of opportunity along the most productive area of the structure. Of course, it requires time on the water to figure all this out. I should also point out that I only anchor if other boats are not drifting through the area. By anchoring, I can hold my position and fish away without making undue noise. When the fish are home, I can usually rely on taking quite a few of them throughout the running tide. Try anchoring and I think you'll find that your fishing will improve in some of these locations. Don't be surprised if you catch some larger fish in these holding areas.

Wading

When wade fishing shallow flats, a quiet approach is the best way to get close-range shots at some of the more traditional shallow-water species including bonefish, permit, and barracuda, and not-so-traditional species like stripers, bluefish, and speckled trout. As previously mentioned, you'll often need to wade downcurrent with the sun at your back for sight fishing. This will help minimize sun glare and put you in a good position to intercept fish swimming upcurrent. *Quiet* is the name of the game when the water may be just inches to a few feet deep. When fish are up on these shallow flats, their senses are on red alert. Any out-of-the-ordinary sight or sound will send them scurrying for the safety of deeper water.

As with any shallow-water situation, fish the water closest to you first. Many flats are approachable by foot. Before plunging in, scan the water's edge and a short distance beyond just in case some fish might be working or holding close by land. While fishing on the little island of Bonaire in the southern Caribbean, I can't tell you how many bonefish were working within 50 feet of the water's edge on a very shallow flat. While wade fishing southern Andros Island in the Bahamas Islands, my fishing partner and excellent caster for the trip, Ted Angradi, hooked a 20-pound-plus 'cuda right at the water's edge. The 'cuda was so intent on getting the fly that it almost beached itself before grabbing the fly and heading for the other side of the bay. Pretty awesome stuff!

When wade fishing, try to minimize noise by moving more slowly and deliberately. This helps minimize the shock waves of sound and water that will be pushed ahead of you as you move, which will alert fish to your presence. If the water is shallow enough, pick your feet up out of the water and slide them back in quietly with each step. This technique is quieter and pushes less water than simply shuffling your feet along, which causes splashes that alert nearby fish. To reduce noise even more in areas of wary fish and soft, sandy bottoms, try wading in shorts and bare feet rather than using wading pants and boots. While wade fishing, your range of sight will be greatly reduced as opposed to fishing from a boat that's elevated above the surface of the water. Therefore, you will need to concentrate on looking for signs of fish within a narrow range extending out only about 30 to 50 feet. Within such close range, you will also be more visible to the fish you are pursuing. If you spot fish approaching or are stalking up on fish, you will need to lower your profile by crouching down and possibly even kneeling to avoid detection.

I was fishing Little Cayman around the fringes of Owen Island, which sits just inside the barrier reef. The tide was dropping and the water was very shallow . . . too shallow for any fish, or so I thought. Suddenly I spotted nervous water just 30 feet away. Bonefish! They were almost on top of me

A quiet low-profile approach is rewarded. First fish the water closest to you, then extend your search. Fish will often station themselves right along the outer edges of grasses waiting for bait to get washed out as the tide recedes.

by the time I saw them. I was standing in just inches of water. Crouching wouldn't do, so I quickly knelt down as low as possible and then hunched over to avoid certain detection by these wary fish. I laid out a very short cast of just 20 feet. The fly touched down softly in front of the approaching pod. Like little fat piglets, the bones fought for first rights to my fly. A few short strips and my line came tight with an 8-pound bone that was just two rod lengths away. The bone still didn't know it was hooked. When I stood up it saw me and shot off like a silver missile across the bay. Wow! In these conditions, stealth is the name of the game.

STAYING IN THE STRIKE ZONE

Whether you're fishing for striped bass, bluefish, or false albacore along the mid-Atlantic coast or bonefish, snook, or tarpon in the Tropics, your odds of success only improve by having your fly stay in the strike zone. This makes perfect sense. If your quarry can't see, hear, or "feel" the presence of your offering, or react fast enough to get it, then you have little hope of the fish accepting your invitation to eat. The strike zone is often defined differently based upon the fish being sought, the fishing situation, and the conditions, but essentially it's the zone or area in which a gamefish will most likely strike your fly. Being in or out of the strike zone can mean the difference between not catching any fish, catching a few, and really hammering them. The following are some effective tactics to use so your fly stays in the strike zone.

First, Find the Strike Zone

Once you've found fish—be it sight fishing in shallow water, fishing in the suds along a beach, or fishing from a boat—your next priority ought to be to find the strike zone in which the fish will feed or strike your fly. There's no sense worrying about whether you have the right fly or retrieve. Even with the right fly and retrieve, the fish will not strike unless you're in the zone.

As discussed earlier in strategy 3, bottom and shoreline structures and features will typically hold fish. These include sloughs, holes, rock piles, shoreline bowls, and rips that are formed by points of land, jetties, bridges, piers, bars, and so on. After locating these, you need to experiment a bit to determine precisely where and how deep fish may be holding. Work these likely fish-holding locations by fan casting the area to ensure you cover it thoroughly. Be sure to present your fly at different depths and with a variety of retrieves (discussed below) before moving on.

When sight fishing in skinny water for species including bones, reds, snook, tarpon, or for that matter stripers, the strike zone is usually almost entirely dependent upon water visibility and the fish's ability to see the fly, and to lesser degree on hearing or "feeling" the fly. In clear water the strike zone may be several feet extending from the sides to the front of the fish. A fly presented 1 or 2 feet in front of a group of cruising bones will almost

Rick Bender works the north side of the Indian River jetty in Delaware. A northeast wind may roil the surf, but is also known for blowing bait to shore and concentrating it against jetties along with gamefish. Strict safety precautions must be observed.

always elicit a strike. The same fly presented the same distance to the side and slightly behind the fish probably won't get a response, or will spook them. In turbid water the strike zone may be reduced to less than 1 foot, or even inches. To complicate matters, most of the time these prized shallow-water species are constantly on the move searching for prey. Therefore, the strike zone is constantly moving. In other situations a bone or redfish may be tilted down rooting around on the bottom and will not see your fly unless you plop it down right on its head. Accurate casting becomes a must in these cases.

PATTERN CASTING

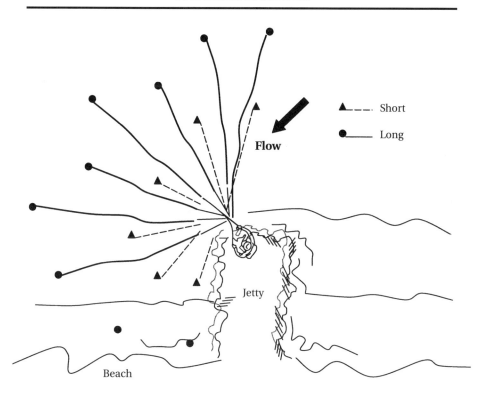

Pattern casting or casting within a wide radius at varying distances is an effective technique for thoroughly searching large areas of water. This technique can be effectively used when fishing from jetties/points of land and while wading along back bays or the beach. Continue pattern casting and varying your retrieve until you locate fish.

Most of the time when fishing in open water for species such as striped bass or bluefish, they are hidden from view and feeding below the surface. The use of a depth- or fish finder is often your best tool to quickly determine the depth and extent of the fish in the area. The depth of the fish will dictate the most appropriate weighted line to use: a floating line for surface-feeding fish, an intermediate line just below the surface, or any of a variety of weighted lines to reach down to 20 feet or more. If you don't have a depth- or fish finder, you'll have to resort to experimentation by casting a weighted line with a known sink rate (say, a 450-grain line with a sink rate of about 8 inches per second), counting down and retrieving at different depths until you get a strike. If you have a fishing buddy or two on board, I recommend you each use different weighted lines and retrieve at different depths to see which works best. Once someone gets a strike, you'll know the approximate depth and can then change lines as needed to get quickly back into the strike zone.

Keep Your Fly in the Water

A basic law of fly fishing is that your fly needs to be in the water to catch fish. While virtually everyone agrees, many anglers do not practice this law to its fullest potential. Call me crazy, but I like to catch fish. Don't get me wrong. Fishing is okay, but for me . . . catching is where it's at. When I'm fishing, I try to maximize the time my fly is in the water. The more time my fly spends in the water, the better my chances are of catching more fish. Over the years I've tried to develop good habits that will increase my odds of success. Having my fly spend more time in the water is one of them.

Here are some ways that you can keep your fly in the water longer:

- Have your rods and reels checked, rigged, and ready to go the night before. Spending time rigging and unrigging on location means you're not fishing. Use rod racks, PVC tubes, or two-piece rod cases to store rods safely during travel. When you arrive at your destination, all you have to do is put the rods together and you're ready.
- Bring multiple rods, reels, and spools (if possible) that are set up for the variety of fishing situations you may encounter during the day. If you have three rods, set up one with an intermediate line, another with a medium-sinking line, and a third with a fast-sinking line. You may also want to have some rods set up with different flies. Capt. Jerry Murphy (Tar-Bone) out of Key Biscayne, Florida, uses an interesting technique.

He has his clients strip out line and sets up coiled line on the deck for two fly rods, one on the port side and one on the starboard. His system works great. You may be fishing with a 7-weight set up with a bonefish fly. If a permit is spotted, you simply put that rod down and pick up the 9-weight set up with a crab pattern. With his setup, you not only have two rods set up with different flies for different scenarios, but the fly line is already stripped out and ready to go. This allows you to switch rods without losing a heartbeat . . . let alone a fish.

- Minimize your false casting. This is critical when sight fishing for bones, tarpon, and even stripers and albies when there is only a very narrow window of opportunity. If your fly is in the air, it's not going to catch a fish. False casting also steals valuable time from fishing. Case in point: A typical eight-hour day striper fishing from a boat may include 500 blind casts. If you were to make 2 extra false casts for every cast, that would equate to an extra 1,000 false casts per day. If each false cast took two seconds, that would mean you lost a total of approximately 33 minutes when your fly wasn't in the water. Remember, if your fly's not in the water, you have no chance of catching a fish.

- Only put a fish on the reel if it earns it. Albies, bones . . . no problem, but if you're catching weakfish, small blues, snook, and especially schoolie-sized stripers, they rarely take any line. Just strip them in by hand. When the fishing gets hot, it usually doesn't last long. You want to take advantage of every second. If you put every fish on the reel, you'll have to take time to strip all that line back out off the reel and false cast a bunch of times to finally get the fly back in the water. On the other hand, if you strip the fish in and release it, you can begin casting immediately and get the fly back in the water much quicker.

- Match the equipment to the size of the fish and fight them correctly to avoid prolonging the battle. You want to enjoy a good tug and be able to land and release fish in good condition. There's been tons of stuff written about this. It makes great sense and also gives you additional time to catch more fish.

Cast Longer with More Accuracy

Yes, you can still catch fish without casting great distances, but I'll guarantee that you'll catch far more fish in many situations if you can cast longer and with more accuracy. This is certainly true in skinny-water situations with spooky fish or when fish are busting just off the beach and the only way to reach them is with a long, accurate cast. If you can't reach the strike zone in these situations, you can forget about catching anything. Longer and more accurate casts are also critical when certain situations present themselves. The sudden swirl or boil of a surface-feeding striper may appear without warning. Your ability to deliver the fly to that small, fleeting strike zone could mean the difference between the catch of the day and the story of the one that got away.

Also, when blind casting from a boat or the beach, longer casts potentially put the fly in front of more fish and in the strike zone longer. Casting longer distances while fishing from a boat also gives you the advantage of getting your fly farther away from any potentially bothersome boat noise. This can give you an added edge in reaching more fish and especially bigger fish that have not been alerted to your presence. I've caught my fair share of big stripers that have taken the fly at the last moment right at the boat. I can also tell you that I've taken many more large stripers on long casts of 70 feet and more. Being capable of casting 70 feet and more versus only 50 feet or less will definitely translate into catching more fish during the course of the day or season.

Fish the Fly at the Right Depth

You can be in the right place but not catch anything because you're not at the right depth. This is especially critical for striped bass when you're fishing bays or offshore. As I mentioned above, you've first got to find the strike zone, and once you find it, you've got to stay in it to consistently catch fish. For example, my fishing buddy Rick Bender and I were fishing the upper Chesapeake in spring. Stripers were showing up on the fish finder from 10 feet down to 20 feet, with the highest concentration being between 18 and 20 feet. I was using a 550-grain weighted line and hooking up every now and then. Rick, on the other hand, had been better prepared. He brought his 850-grain shooting-head system and was hooking up with much greater consistency. Rick was not only able to get his fly down to the primary strike zone quicker than I, but his fly stayed in that deeper strike zone longer. The results? Rick caught more and bigger fish, including a nice 20-pounder.

The ideal situation is to use a weighted line that will enable you to simply cast and begin retrieving the fly through the primary strike zone. My experience is that this often requires a willingness to throw a heavier line than you

LONGER CASTS GIVE FLIES MORE STRIKE-ZONE EXPOSURE

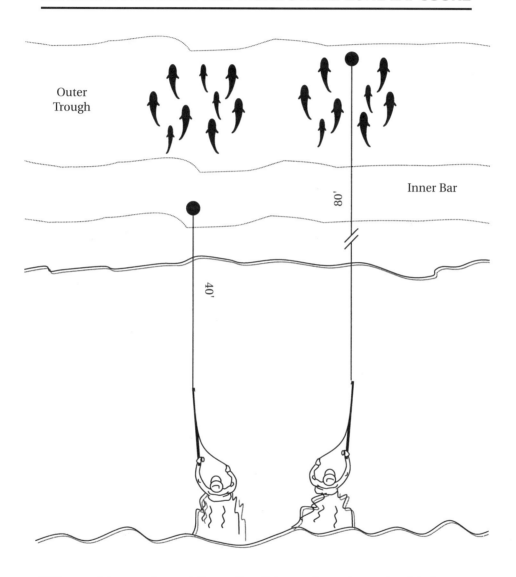

With everything equal except the casting distance, the angler on the right has excellent hook-up potential, while the angler on the left has little, if any. In many fishing situations, especially when blind casting in open water or along beaches, longer casts will often put your fly in front of more fish more often. Your odds of success will increase dramatically.

GETTING DOWN INTO THE STRIKE-ZONE

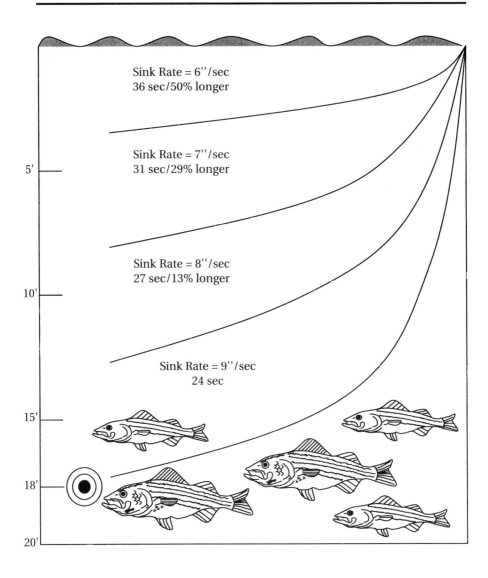

As you can readily see from this illustration, not only are sinking lines essential in getting to the strike zone (18 feet), they also get your fly there faster. Less waiting while your fly is sinking means you can make more casts to the strike zone, thus increasing hook-up potential.

might prefer. For instance, I would prefer to cast a lighter 350-grain line and would probably catch fish. However, if I were to switch to a heavier 450-grain line, I would not have to wait as long for the line to sink and could begin retrieving almost immediately with more consistent hook-ups.

Shorten and Slow Down the Retrieve

I don't know about you, but when I cast into breaking stripers, blues, or albies my heart starts racing and I have a tendency to start ripping the fly through the water. This may work with very high concentrations of breaking fish, but some very frustrating experiences have taught me to shorten and slow down the retrieves for more consistent hook-ups. During my early experiences with albies in the Cape Lookout area of North Carolina, fish were chasing bait at the surface in small groups of three or four fish. I could get the cast quickly to the boils, but would strip the fly like a madman right out of the strike zone in all the excitement. What an idiot! I'd come up empty each time. Talk about being frustrated. Once I realized what was happening, I would make the cast to the boils, resist the urge, and let it sit for a second or two. If I didn't have a strike, I would usually just have to twitch it a few short inches to entice a take. What a huge difference. Shorter, slower retrieves also work especially well for stripers when fishing below the surface and when down deep. If you're marking lots of fish on the fish finder and you feel the fly is right in their midst, don't be too anxious. Bigger stripers usually hang under the smaller, more active fish just waiting for some tasty morsels to slowly drift down. Slow down your retrieve and you might just be in for a surprise.

Don't Yank the Fly Away

Experienced flats fishermen learn not to yank the fly away early on or be faced with going insane from missed opportunities. This can be about as frustrating as it gets for an angler. There you are on the flats with a beautiful 10-pound bone or 20-pound striper in plain view not 50 feet away. You make a great presentation. The fly gently touches down a foot or two in front of the fish. A few short strips, and the fly has the attention of the fish. The fish sips the fly in, and you feel some slight resistance. With your heart pounding, you make a long strip-strike (see strategy 6) and raise your rod with great anticipation of coming tight against the weight of that magnificent fish. To your total disappointment and utter dismay, you feel nothing as you watch your fly leap from the fish's mouth and land some 10 or 15 feet away. The fish can't find the fly that escaped its grasp and swims away out of range. Avoid this unfortunate scenario by just varying your striking technique and controlling the emotions that run so high in these situations.

While the flats fisherman often sees this entire scenario unfold before his eyes, that's not to say that very similar occurrences aren't happening to

Big stripers will often hold under smaller schooling fish waiting for tasty morsels to drift down. This 40-inch late December striper was taken down deep in 25 feet of water using a very slow retrieve while fishing off the beaches of Seaside Park New Jersey,

those of us fishing in deeper and/or more turbid water even though we can't see our fly or the fish. Opportunities for catching stripers, sea trout, blues, or albies can also be lost by making too long a strip-strike and raising the rod at the same time. It's not so much that you missed the hookup—we all do that on occasion. Rather, it's that by making a very long, hard strip-strike, perhaps in combination with raising the rod, the fly is pulled far away and out of the fish's strike zone. If the fish can't find the fly, you won't get a second chance. Most saltwater species are used to getting stuck by sharp things on a regular basis by the foods they eat. So although a fish may have felt the hook, it will often eat the fly again providing it's still in the strike zone. Many times the second take of the fly will be more aggressive than the first, since the fish thought it was about to get away. In the case of schooling fish like stripers or blues, there may be other fish in the vicinity. If your fly is pulled only a short distance away, another fish may quickly seize the opportunity and snatch your fly. Try keeping your strip-strikes short and not too hard, and don't raise your rod. Keep it pointing at the fish. Once you feel the weight of the fish, you may want to make a few short rapid strikes to set the hook firmly, then raise the rod. This technique is very applicable when fishing for bonefish, permit, and redfish.

Use Anchors

When fishing from a boat in search of schooling fish or working structure like bridges, rock piles, or ledges, I normally don't like using an anchor simply because eventually I'll have to pull it in, which requires some effort. Drifting is usually a productive way to do most fishing. However, there are situations around structures like these, where the use of an anchor is extremely effective in allowing you to work over the structure much more thoroughly. By doing so, you spend less time repositioning the boat for each drift. Often you can only catch a fish or two before having to reposition for another drift. On the other hand, by anchoring you have more time to fish and can do a much better job getting the fly to the most productive features of the structure.

Another type of anchor that is also very effective in keeping you in the strike zone longer is the sea anchor. This is essentially a large, flexible funnel with a line tied off to the boat. The sea anchor causes drag and slows down the boat's drift in fast current or on windy days, enabling you to stay over fish longer. It also has another benefit. Because the sea anchor reduces your drift speed, sinking lines are more likely to stay down where the fish are and in the strike zone.

EFFECTIVE PRESENTATIONS

As I mentioned in the introduction, about 90 percent of the fish are caught by only 10 percent of the anglers. Obviously, those 10 percent are doing a variety of things differently. I'd like to share with you some effective fly presentations that have made the difference for me in a variety of fly-fishing situations. Besides being able to locate fish and select the correct fly, the ability and willingness to vary the way you present your fly is one of the most important tactics for getting more strikes.

Before we turn to different presentations, there are a few things to keep in mind when you're fishing. First, you must always remember to keep in touch with your fly. If there is too much slack in your line, you often won't be able to feel a soft take and won't be able to properly set the hook. To avoid this you should keep your rod tip pointed down, just off or even slightly below the surface of the water. Keeping the rod tip just under the surface when making rapid retrieves will prevent the fly line from wrapping around the end of the rod tip while retreiving. Besides keeping your

Anchoring the boat at the edge of a mangrove inlet permits anglers to work the area effectively without boat noise spooking the fish. Here fly anglers are picking off the snook that are holding at the mouth of a creek during the falling tides.

rod pointed down, also keep it pointed straight toward your fly. With a straight rod and fly line, slack will be minimized. If a fish takes your fly, you'll be perfectly poised to feel the take and set the hook.

There are two basic methods of retrieving the fly: one-handed and two-handed. The one-handed retrieve is essentially the same technique that you would use to strip in and retrieve your fly line using your nonrod hand. The difference in this case is that instead of just stripping in your fly line, you are imparting action to the fly and making it look alive. To be more successful, don't think of it as just stripping in fly line; think of it as making your fly mimic the darting or swimming motion of a baitfish, crab, or shrimp. Make your fly dance, make it come alive. It is very important to maintain proper line control with your rod hand while retrieving your fly. As you strip down with your nonrod hand, relieve the tension on the fly line with your rod hand so it slips smoothly between your fingers and the rod handle. At the end of each strip, put tension back on the fly line with your rod hand while you reposition your nonrod hand for the next strip retrieve. This technique will ensure proper line control in case a fish strikes. If your line is loose, you may not detect subtle strikes.

The two-handed retrieve is slightly different in that you will need to tuck the rod handle up under the crux of your armpit and hold it there as you retrieve. This frees both hands for retrieving. With your rod tip pointing down or at the surface, alternate grabbing the fly line with one hand then the other and strip in your fly. The two-handed retrieve allows you more control over your fly. You can strip faster or at a steady pace with two hands.

Steady Retrieve

The steady or regular retrieve is used by most anglers most of the time. The retrieve is typically a consistent or steady stripping action of about 6 to 10 inches in length. You can vary the retrieving speed anywhere from slow to fairly fast while fishing, but the overall action is usually consistent within any one cast. When fish are aggressive and not very finicky, this retrieve may be all that's needed for consistent hook-ups. The downside is that you can fall into a rut of relying on it too much for most of your fishing. This can lead to a significant decrease in strikes and frustration when fish are less aggressive and looking for something different to come along. Here are nine effective retrieves that you can use and combine for a variety of angling situations to increase your odds of success.

DEAD DRIFTING AND SWINGING AROUND STRUCTURE

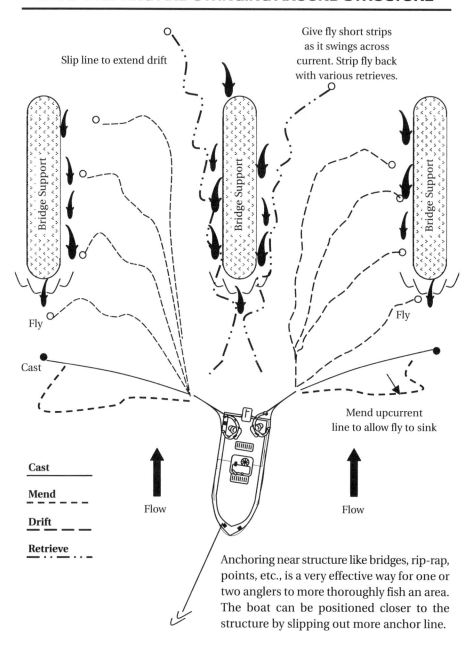

Slip line to extend drift

Give fly short strips as it swings across current. Strip fly back with various retrieves.

Bridge Support

Bridge Support

Bridge Support

Fly

Fly

Cast

Mend upcurrent line to allow fly to sink

Cast

Mend

Drift

Retrieve

Flow

Flow

Anchoring near structure like bridges, rip-rap, points, etc., is a very effective way for one or two anglers to more thoroughly fish an area. The boat can be positioned closer to the structure by slipping out more anchor line.

Rapid Fire

The rapid fire is a great retrieve that often entices fish to strike when other retrieves, especially the steady strip, just aren't making it happen. The strikes are usually violent. For this retrieve, try to strip the fly as short and as fast as you can. Basically it's a 1- to 3-inch rapid retrieving action. Just picture the fly in the water going crazy in rapid up-and-down motions like an injured baitfish that's going spastic. Another side benefit is that since the stripping action is very short, the fly stays in the strike zone longer. Many gamefish often find the rapid-fire retrieve irresistible.

Rip and Pause

Stripers, snook and other gamefish will often follow a fly all the way back to the boat without the angler ever knowing it. When the steady/regular and rapid-fire retrieves aren't producing strikes on a frequent basis and you suspect there are fish in the area, it's time for a change. A few years ago I was fishing on the upper Chesapeake with my friend Ken Steffen, who is an avid trout fly fisherman but was new to striper fishing. We were getting only a few strikes, yet I believed we had a fair amount of fish around the boat right by a drop-off. I began to explain to Ken that if stripers are following the fly they will often be enticed to strike when there is a rapid speedup, followed by a definitive pause. As I explained the technique, Ken was trying to perform it, and when he came to the pause . . . wham! A striper slammed his fly. Ken was hooked up!

This is a great technique especially when fishing deeper water with a weighted line and fly like a Clouser Minnow or Jiggy Fly. I believe the technique is effective because the fast ripping motion of the fly gets the attention of the fish. The fish begins to track the fly but, for whatever reason, doesn't seem interested enough to strike. When the angler pauses, the weighted fly dips sharply, resembling an injured baitfish. By this time the fish is so charged up that it instinctively strikes the fly.

Dead Drifting

This presentation technique is quite different from the two just discussed. Instead of actively retrieving your fly, dead drifting requires that you take a passive approach and let your fly drift along a current seam as if dead, stunned, or dying. Dead drifting is a very effective technique for presenting your fly to species such as striped bass, sea trout, and snook that use currents to carry bait to their holding positions. If you have nymph fished for trout, you are already familiar with the technique. It requires that you typically cast across current and mend or reposition the line upcurrent to allow the fly/line to sink and be carried along with the flow. Actually, the cast can be placed anywhere from 45 degrees across and upcurrent to 45 degrees across and downcurrent, depending upon where you suspect the fish are holding, your location, and their relative depth. Casting across and upcurrent will permit more time for your fly/line to sink—providing, of course, that you keep mending upcurrent to minimize drag.

Unlike nymph fishing for trout, I don't feel having a totally drag-free drift is entirely necessary or desirable in saltwater fly fishing. I have found that an occasional short strip or twitch of the rod will trigger strikes. Some fish can become particularly selective and will only take flies on a dead drift within a very specific area or strike zone. When dead drifting, it is very important that you minimize slack line and follow the drift with your rod tip so that you can feel and/or see your line for any indications of a strike.

Swinging

Swinging your fly is achieved by casting directly across current to 45 degrees downcurrent. Instead of using an upcurrent mend, as in dead drifting, a downcurrent mend is used for swinging to intentionally create drag. The drag that is created causes the fly to accelerate and swing sideways across and downcurrent from your position. Swinging the fly at different angles, depths, and distances is a very effective technique to fish a location. A fly swung across a current provides a wide side profile of your fly and increases the likelihood that any fish in the area will see it. Many strikes occur just when the swing straightens out. A few short strips at this time will usually entice fish to strike your fly. Using dead drifting with swinging can be a very effective combination. By feeding additional fly line and even backing during the dead-drifting stage, you can greatly extend the area that you wish to cover.

The Drop-Back

There are lessons to be learned from all types of fishing other than fly fishing. I learned years ago as a kid while bottom fishing for carp that if you happen to finally get a bite but miss the hook-up, don't be foolish and yank the dinner plate away when somebody's trying to eat . . . give it back. Many anglers only think of retrieving the fly in one direction—namely, back to the angler—and miss out on some outstanding opportunities. While I was fall striper fishing with some friends off southern New Jersey, we located some stripers that were down deep in about 20 to 25 feet of water. It wasn't a large concentration of fish, so it would be important to make every cast count once the fly finally got down to the depth the fish were holding at. I was using a 550-grain sinking-tip line and made a cast of only about 40 or 50 feet upcurrent and upwind. To ensure that the line continued to sink, I fed

EFFECTIVE FLY RETRIEVES

Side View of Retrieving Action

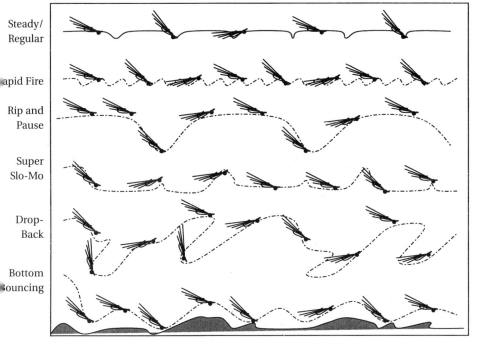

Steady/
Regular

apid Fire

Rip and
Pause

Super
Slo-Mo

Drop-
Back

Bottom
ouncing

Overhead View of Retrieving Action

Wiggle-
Waggle

out about another 60 feet of slack line over the course of 40 seconds or so. On the third strip of my retrieve, I felt a fish take the fly, but wasn't able to set the hook. Instead of retrieving the fly back to the boat, I quickly fed out about 10 feet of slack line and dropped the fly back to the fish. I started my retrieve again and on the second strip I was tight to a nice striper.

Having to retrieve the fly all the way back to the boat in order to get the fly back in the water exactly where I just pulled it from didn't make a whole lot of sense. The right technique to use in this situation was the drop-back retrieve. Think of it as a retrieve in reverse. The fly still has fish-attraction power going down and away, perhaps even more. When you miss a hook-up, all you need to do is drop the rod tip and feed out several feet of slack line. Wait a moment until it comes tight, and then twitch it slightly. Stripers will often follow the fly as it drops back, and the moment it's moved they'll often suck it back in their mouths. Keep in mind that stripers and other fish with sizable mouths can suck even a very large fly in and out in just a fraction of a second. All you may feel is a slight bump. That was the take. When you feel the take, make a short strip-strike to see if you're hooked up. If not, just repeat it a few more times. Be patient, keep the fly in the strike zone, and you may rewarded.

Bottom Bouncing

As you probably know, fish will often hug the bottom around structure. Getting the fly down on the bottom where the fish are is key. Sometimes fish will strike only when the fly is actually bouncing off the bottom. This can occur in deep as well as fairly shallow water. You'll know your fly is on the bottom when you feel it tapping, or when it occasionally gets hooked on something like clam- or oyster shells. While fishing in shallow water of 2 or 3 feet in the middle Chesapeake near Tilgham Island, I would get most of my strikes immediately after the fly pulled loose from an oyster shell. Bottom bouncing was also very effective a few summers ago when I was fishing for huge 4- to 6-pound croakers off the beaches of Cape Charles, Virginia.

Water Slap

When faced with unusual fishing conditions, sometimes you have to abandon traditional techniques and try something radically different. The results may surprise you. Here's an example. I was fishing the Chesapeake and had been doing quite well on subsurface stripers using a sinking line when the wind suddenly began to blow very hard. As the boat drifted, I continued to cast upstream and upwind. Casting the large 8- to 10-inch herring imitation became increasingly difficult as the gusts exceeded 15 knots while my hook-ups all but disappeared. As I looked around on my backcast I noticed boils within 10 to 25 feet of the downstream side of the boat. The wind had whipped up the water to a nice 1½-foot chop that apparently confused the baitfish and turned on the stripers.

Stripers that had been feeding lower in the water column were now feeding just below the surface, but casting into the wind was exceedingly difficult and tiresome with the large fly. With the fish feeding aggressively so close to the boat, I decided to try something a little radical. I reeled in until I only had 20 to 25 feet of line outside the rod tip that I could pick up and put down easily. I then turned and faced downwind and cast the fly—or should I say *smacked* the fly on the surface hard and paused for a brief moment. If I didn't get a strike, I then picked up the fly and just smacked it down again without any retrieve. On the third cast a nice 5- or 6-pound striper took the fly. It worked! After releasing the fish, I smacked the fly again on the water not 20 feet from the boat. The water exploded when a 16-pound striper engulfed the fly. What a surprise! The water slap has worked equally well fishing just off the New Jersey shore when surface-feeding stripers and blues would come near the boat. No need to cast very far in these situations. More often than not, the sound and commotion of the fly smacking the water triggers a strike.

Wiggle-Waggle

The wiggle-waggle is a retrieving technique imparted by your rod rather than your hands. The technique involves a slight side-to-side motion with the rod tip as you're retrieving your fly. As a result, the fly gets a little extra wiggle or waggle that apparently turns on otherwise finicky fish. This is also an excellent technique to use when dead drifting. Stripers and sea trout often follow a drifting fly. Sometimes they'll readily sip it in, but in other situations they'll be hesitant. A little wiggle-waggle gives the fly just a little "shimmer" of life that often makes them commit. What I especially like about the wiggle-waggle is that it can be used in conjunction with many of the other types of retrieves mentioned above.

Super Slo-Mo

When water temperatures fall, fish can become more lethargic. After you've tried all the other retrieves without much success, try one more—the super slo-mo. This is a retrieve that can save the day. It's not just slow, but a super-slow-motion retrieve; very slight twitches combined with big *looooong* pauses. When you think you can't go any slower, go even slower. With a very slow retrieve your fly stays in front of the fish longer to tease them into taking. In these situations, the take may be very subtle. You may only feel a slight bump, so be prepared to strike. Slowing things down can really pay off. Sometimes the best retrieve is almost no retrieve.

There are probably as many different presentation techniques as there are anglers. Use what works, but when it doesn't, be willing to vary your presentation. Be creative, try something different, and you may just be surprised at the results you get.

SHORT PRECISION CASTING TO SMALL PODS OF FISH ON THE MOVE

When fishing for open-water species such as stripers, bluefish, Spanish macs, bonito, and false albacore, remember that these fish are not always found in large surface-feeding schools where a "close enough" cast is good enough. Often these fish can be found in smaller pods that are constantly on the move and popping up here and then there. To catch these fish, precision casting is required. The window of opportunity is a small one, and if a cast is going to successful, it has to be accurate, not just close enough. This strategy involves making short precision casts directly to spots where fish are actively feeding or chasing bait. This is not much different from the scenarios encountered by flats anglers. Many of the signs are similar to those for the flats. The fish in deeper water will pop bait at the surface, wake, boil, roll, and push bait out of the water in front of them. The big difference, though, is that these fish are often moving quite fast. Accurate casts are very important in these situations, but they have to be made to where a fish is or is going, not to where it was.

What I have discovered while fishing for stripers, bluefish, and especially false albacore is that you must direct your cast to where the action currently is or is likely to be. Let me explain. If you just chuck a cast out to the action that just occurred—such as surface busts, finning, or boils—it may be too late. The fish have probably already moved on. This is fine for larger slower-moving schools of fish, but smaller pods of fish move and often move fast. This happens frequently with stripers in the Chesapeake Bay when pods are mixed with faster species like blues and Spanish macs and along the Atlantic with blues and albies. The pods seem to move as fast as the fastest fish, which pushes them along at a pretty fast clip. It's amazing how fast you have get the boat going to cut them off and get in position to get a shot.

In these situations, I'll have an angler set up in the bow of the boat and will have him strip out enough line to make a 35- to 40-foot cast. Too much line usually spells tangles and disaster. He will also have about 15 feet of line outside the rod tip to load the rod quickly and will have the fly pinched between his forefinger and thumb ready for a speed cast, discussed earlier. I'll run ahead of the fish and make a hard turn at a right angle (left or right) to cut the fish off at the pass. The more typical cautious approach where the boat is positioned upstream/upwind ahead of the fish and drifting up on them usually does not work in these situations, since the fish usually move on too quickly and change direction. If you're good, you'll get maybe one cast before the fish are out of range. This is very frustrating. If you use what I call a quick-T approach in positioning the boat, you'll be in an excellent position to make a short, accurate cast. Once the boat is turned into the fish, the engine is cut off and the boat should be allowed to drift into position to intercept the fish. The angler set up in the bow needs to be alert and ready to cast. It is very important that he *wait* and not cast until he sees fish signs close to the boat. You do not want to just blind cast in these situations. Often what happens is the angler is excited with anticipation and makes a long cast, 60 feet or more, to the action that *was* taking place. Unfortunately, as soon as the angler makes the long cast, fish pop up within 30 feet of the boat, but the angler cannot recast until he retrieves most of the line. By that time the fish are often gone. To avoid this scenario, the angler in the bow should only cast to fish that can be seen actively boiling and busting on bait close to the boat. He should make a quick cast and put the fly right into the middle of the action. It's important that the fly be left in the action and *not* stripped out of the strike zone. You want the fly to represent a wounded baitfish. If your fly is not taken, give it a few short strips to see if you get some interest. If not, another cast into nearby action may be needed.

While in these rather hectic situations, it's important to stay alert to other signs of where the fish are. If a pod of fish drops out of sight, look for

other clues such as a lead bird flying close to the water and dipping occasionally or a spray of bait erupting from the surface. If you see these signs,
direct your cast slightly ahead of the bait or bird (6 to 8 feet). This should
put your fly directly in the path of the moving fish. A few short twitches and
your fly should attract some immediate attention. These short precision
casts have proven very effective for fast-moving pods of false albacore,
stripers, blues, and Spanish macs.

THE QUICK T APPROACH

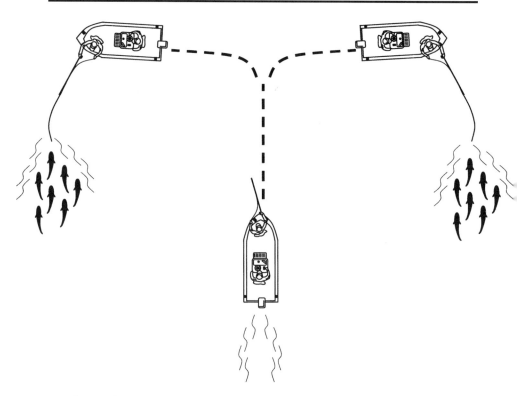

Use the quick T approach for spooky and fast-moving fish like false albacore, bluefish, Spanish macs, etc., that provide only a quick window of opportunity to make
a cast. Determine the path and intercept fish by watching for clues including surface disturbances, fleeing bait, and leading birds. Be prepared to make a quick
speed cast and deliver the fly to surface action or just ahead of fleeing bait or birds.

DO WHAT THE FISH TELL YOU

No matter what type of fish you're targeting and no matter what fly or re-trieve you're using, you must always do one important thing— do what the fish tell you. Of course we all know that fish can't talk, but they can still communicate very effectively by means of their behavior. In order to be even more effective as an angler you'll need to train yourself first to ac-tively look for clues to observable fish behavior, and second to understand what course of action you'll need to take.

Here's an example to illustrate what I'm talking about.

It was midspring in Jersey and my friend Rick Bender and I were fishing Barnegat Bay from my boat for big tiderunner weakfish or sea trout. The wind was blowing hard out of the southeast at about 15 to 18 mph, and it whipped the shallow bay into a pretty good froth with 1- to 2-foot rollers. Gray sea trout or weakies, as we call them in Jersey, usually can be found on or near the bottom. With slightly turbid conditions and a water depth between 6 and 8 feet, we started out with 350-grain sinking line and 5- to 6-inch yellow-over-white Jiggy Flies developed by Bob Popovics. The fly simulated silversides, the predominant bait this time of year. Usually Bob's Jiggy is a consistent producer for these early-spring fish. Our strat-egy was to put the fly right down at the bottom and in the strike zone of the weakfish.

We were still in our first drift when Rick shouted out that he had just seen a big weakie surfing in the waves; it had made a move on the fly but missed. I've fished enough with Rick to know that he has fantastic vision and is a great observer. I had not observed any fish, but if Rick said he saw a surfing weakie, by God that's what he saw. The words weren't even out of Rick's mouth before we were both reeling in and grabbing for our other rods, already set up with clear intermediate lines and one of my Pretender Silverside simulators. This is a great fly for simulating silversides, especially with the Mylar pearlescent tubing that gives the fly silver flash on the sides. More importantly, the Mylar simulates the opaque truncated stomach sac of silversides, especially when backlit at the surface. The fly was a perfect choice. On my third cast I came tight to a beautiful 8- or 9-

pound tiderunner. Over the course of the next few hours, Rick and I both would land and lose several more of these beautiful fish.

In this scenario, we started out with weighted lines and flies for the early-spring tiderunners, which is typical for this time of year. However, the observable behavior of the fish told us, "Hey dummies, we're up top surfing these waves for silversides." Rick and I may be dumb, but we're not stupid. We didn't waste a heartbeat switching over to the clear intermediate fly line and a more buoyant fly that would suspend in the water column and stay in the strike zone near the water's surface. We observed, we listened, and we were rewarded.

By keeping alert, you'll be more likely to detect the presence of gamefish and note whether or not they have an interest in your offering. A quality pair of polarized sunglasses will enable you to see into the water. Watch to see if fish are following your fly. If the water is clear and there is sufficient light, you may be able to peer through the water and see the actual fish or catch the glimpse of a flash. A swirl, a boil, or a push of water near your fly may also give a fish's presence away. If it's not willing to commit to striking your fly, it's telling you to try something different. Here are some fast and simple changes that may trigger strikes:

- Change your retrieve from fast to slow and steady or from slow to fast and erratic.
- Shorten your leader if you're fishing a sinking line.
- Lengthen your leader if you're fishing a floating or intermediate line.
- Use a lighter tippet.
- Change from a large fly to a small one, or from a small fly to a large one.
- If your brightly colored fly is being refused, try a dark fly and vice versa.
- Switch from a nonweighted fly to a weighted one or vice versa.
- If you've been fishing below the surface, try fishing poppers, sliders, or Crease Flies at the surface or vice versa.
- Change from a floating line to an intermediate or to a sinking line or vice versa.

Your success can often be increased through close observation of fish behavior coupled with a willingness to change your angling strategies. This may also include fishing in a different location if it's just not happening at your present spot.

Finding quiet waters, for example, is a great strategy to use when fish get turned off by a lot of boat noise. The fish are telling you, "We're not eating, guys. Better try somewhere else." Many boat anglers won't risk leaving the fleet for fear of losing out. Losing out on what? If most of the boats in a fleet are hooking up with consistency, I would be hesitant to leave also. However, take your binoculars out and take a look around. I think you'll often find that most of the boats are not catching a thing. I'd rather risk not catching than put up with mayhem. If you decide to leave the fleet, maybe you won't find as large a concentration of fish, but what's the difference if they have lockjaw? A quieter stretch of water away from the fleet and all that boat noise may have less fish, but the fish you'll find will often be much more cooperative.

Similarly, if the surf fishing is slow along your favorite stretch of beach, try fishing the bay, an inlet, or a new section of beach that you haven't tried before. These are great times to venture out on your own and learn new waters. Your odds of success may actually increase, and you may discover that new "secret spot." Just remember that not all waters are productive all

A large tiderunner weakfish feeding near the surface locked onto Mike's Silverside Pretender (fluorescent yellow over white). With a fair amount of flash, the Pretender doubles as a simulator and attractor pattern, especially when small rattles are inserted in the piping.

the time. The time you spend on the water will begin to reveal mysteries—which to me can be more rewarding than catching fish. Nothing ventured . . . nothing gained.

STRATEGY 5—MAXIMIZE YOUR PRESENTATION

Anglers who are routinely successful have learned to maximize their presentation. You'll need to do the same if you wish to be successful too.

- Use the right fly line:
  Floating.
  Intermediate.
  Sinking.
- Leaders function by:
  Keeping your fly line connected to your fly/fish.
  Turning your fly over.
  Providing an "invisible" connection to your fly line.
  Providing distance between your fly and fly line.
  Imparting the right action to the fly.
  Keeping your fly tracking at the same depth as your fly line.
- Approach your quarry carefully by boat and by wading.
- Stay in the strike zone with your fly.
- Retrieve your fly effectively to entice strikes.
- Use short precision casting to small pods of fish on the move.
- Do what the fish tell you.

HOOK UP AND STAY HOOKED

E ven the best of anglers will lose an occasional fish, but some anglers, especially novices, can't seem to stay hooked. I'm sure most anglers would agree that fishing is great, but catching is where it's at. The following are some important tactics that will help you get hooked up and stay hooked.

HOOKS

This is the business end of your fishing equipment. As such, I recommend using good-quality stainless-steel (s/s) hooks. They'll be more reliable in a tug-of-war and won't rust so you can use them again and again. You'll need to consider the size of the fly you will be tying and the size of the fish's mouth. Surprisingly, saltwater fish usually aren't hook-shy, so you needn't worry about getting refused because your hook is a little too large. It's far more important to consider the hook's effect on the fly's action. For example, you should use a hook of a thinner/lighter wire to reduce weight for topwater flies like poppers, sliders, and Crease Flies and for flies that you want to suspend like the Deceivers or Pretenders discussed in strategy 4. Thicker/heavier hooks work well for flies that will be worked deep or that will have a jigging action, like Clouser Deep Minnows or Jiggy Flies. When fishing for big fish with big mouths like tarpon, snook, and stripers that often feed on larger prey, large flies (4 to 8 inches or more) on larger hooks from sizes 1/0 to 4/0 are typically used. For fish with smaller mouths like redfish, bonefish, false albacore, and sea trout that feed on smaller prey, smaller hooks from sizes 8 to 1 are typically used. This is not to say that very large tarpon or stripers won't take a fly as small as a 6 . . . they will when the predominant bait is small. Conversely, false albacore are typically caught on small silverside and rainbait imitations in the 2 to 6 hook-size range. However, when they are feeding on by-catch or mullet, I have taken them on the Pretender Mullet pattern up to 7 or 8 inches in length on a 4/0 hook.

Saltwater fish pull much harder than most freshwater fish. Pressure of 10 to 15 pounds or more may be exerted while fighting powerful fish. An important consideration when tying any fly is to ensure that there is a sufficient hook gap. Too narrow a hook gap can result in missed hook-ups or lost fish because the hook had a weak hold. Avoid these problems by tying flies so that excess body materials won't interfere with the hook gap and/or by selecting a slightly larger-sized hook, but one that won't interfere with the fly's action.

Whatever hooks you use, make sure they are sharp. The point should be sharpened on three sides like a triangle with a hook-sharpening file that can be purchased at your local fly shop. This provides a sharp point as well as three sharp edges to help drive the hook home solidly, even in the hard mouths of tarpon. If I have to sharpen my hooks, I do so before I tie my flies. I forget enough things. With my hooks already sharpened, I'll have one less thing to worry about. You also won't have all the fly-tying materials getting in the way. A number of manufacturers now offer chemically sharpened hooks. These are very sharp and work well.

This is a good place to also talk about barbed versus barbless hooks. When I sharpen my hooks (sizes 2 and up) before tying, I also use pliers to mash down the barbs. I leave the barb on the smaller hooks because I feel the hook is small and will penetrate easily even with the barb up. Also, I feel the smaller hooks could use a little help holding on; in the smaller sizes, I don't feel the fish gets injured seriously. How's the holding ability of the larger hooks with the barbs mashed down? I think they hold just fine, and they minimize injury to the fish. I lose very few fish during the course of a year. When I do lose one, it usually has more to do with not keeping a tight line than it does with not having a barb. I look at it this way: Better to lose a few fish than to possibly injure many others.

Before tying on any fly, check the point to make sure it's very sharp. You can do this simply by dragging the hook point across your thumbnail. If it bites into your nail easily, it's plenty sharp. If not, hit a few times on each of the three edges with a file. If you're fishing around rocks or hard sandy bottoms with shells, check your fly periodically to make sure the point is still nice and sharp. Additionally, if you happen to miss hooking up or have a fish come off, take time out and check your fly. The point may have dulled or even become bent. Sometimes you may only get a few strikes in a day. You don't want to lose them because your hook point wasn't sharp.

KNOTS/CONNECTIONS

Keep in mind that you must stay connected to stay in the game. If not . . . game over! The knots you use to connect your fly to the end of your leader must be strong, reliable, and have a breaking strength that is at or close to the strength of the line. For example, if you were bonefishing with some reasonably small flies (sizes 4 to 6), you would want to use a lighter tippet of, say, 10-pound test. A tippet weight of 10-pound test would be flexible enough to impart the proper action to the fly while still strong enough for an angler to exert sufficient pressure to land the fish. This, of course, is not just dependent on the pound test of the tippet. It is also dependent upon the strength of the knot you tie. With a tippet weight of 10-pound test, the maximum pressure you could expect to put on a fish is 10 pounds. However, your knots or connections are with few exceptions the weakest link in your system. So in reality, while you may have a tippet of 10-pound test, you will only be able to exert about 8 or 9 pounds of pressure before your connection would fail. And that's assuming you're using and tying good knots. Even 8 or 9 pounds of pressure is still quite a bit of pressure to exert on a fish. In my experience, most saltwater fly fishermen rarely ever put that much pressure on their fish.

I like to keep this knot stuff simple, so I'm going to review the knots I use and have found to be reliable for me. All of them are tied with variations on an overhand knot. Since anyone can tie an overhand knot, you'll be able to easily tie these. Other folks may have their favorites, but these are mine. They have been used time and time again with success on such tough saltwater species as large double-digit bonefish with their blistering runs, stripers and redfish that can really bulldog, and false albacore in the 16- to 18-pound range that possess both speed and unwavering stamina.

You need to be aware of a few things when tying knots:

- Use more twists with lighter/smaller-diameter lines and fewer twists for heavier/larger-diameter lines.
- Always cinch down each knot good and tight. Knots that slip under pressure most often fail, and you wind up with a broken connection and a lost fish. Lighter lines can be pulled tight easily with your hands. Heavier lines need to be pulled tight with the aid of a pair of pliers or by placing a loop knot over a fixed object or the handle of your scissors or pliers.
- Before you cinch down your knots, wet them first with saliva for lubrication to reduce friction. This is important. If a knot is not lubricated, a significant amount of friction may be created, causing excessive heat and possible damage to the line and connection. The connection may look all right, but it may have been weakened from the heat and may break when challenged by a good fish.
- Cinch down and gradually pull each knot tight as instructed. For many knots, it may be important to hold both ends of the line and tag ends when tightening, as with double surgeon's and blood knots.
- For extra strength, add a small drop of cyanoacrylate (Zap-A-Gap) to the connection to prevent the knot from slipping.
- Finally, always test your connections by giving them a good hard pull. Better it break now than when you have a good fish on.

Let's review each connection or knot starting from the fly/hook and working back.

Connecting Tippet to Hook

NONSLIP MONO LOOP KNOT

This is a great knot with superior knot strength; it's easy to tie and allows your fly to move around to enhance action. As the name implies, the knot is nonslip so you avoid the problems inherent in other knots that may slip. Unless I'm using very heavy tippet, I use this knot almost exclusively to attach my flies.

HOW TO TIE First, tie an overhand knot about 3 or 4 inches up from the end of the tippet, but be sure to keep it slightly open. Next, feed the 3- to 4-inch tag end through the eye of the hook and then through the overhand knot you just tied. Grab the tag end and wrap it around the long end of the tippet four or five times. You'll need to wrap it more times for lighter lines, and fewer the heavier the line gets. Five wraps is good for up to 17-pound-test tippet; four wraps is good for 20- to 40-pound test. Then push the tag end back through the overhand knot the same way. Gradually pull the tag end and the long end of the tippet in opposite directions at the same time until cinched all the way down. Trim the tag end. For heavier lines, use a pair of pliers to pull the tag end tight.

NONSLIP MONO LOOP KNOT

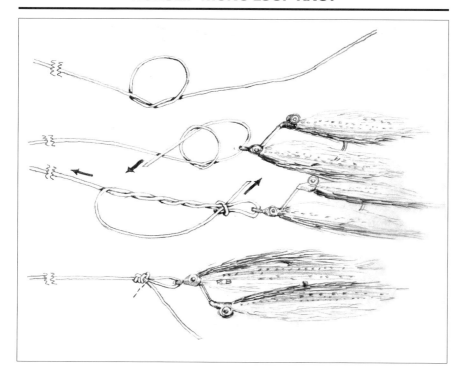

Connecting Heavy Shock Tippet to Hook

HOMER RHODE LOOP KNOT

This is another loop knot, but it's generally used for heavy shock tippet.

HOW TO TIE Start by tying an overhand knot about 3 or 4 inches up from the end of the line. Take the short tag end and run it through the eye of the hook and then through the overhand knot you just tied. Then cinch the first overhand knot down, but not all the way. Now pull the tippet so the first knot slides down to the eye of the hook. Next, with the short tag end, tie a second overhand knot around the tippet and snug up, but not all the way. Remember that the distance from the eye of the hook to where you tie the

HOMER RHODE LOOP KNOT

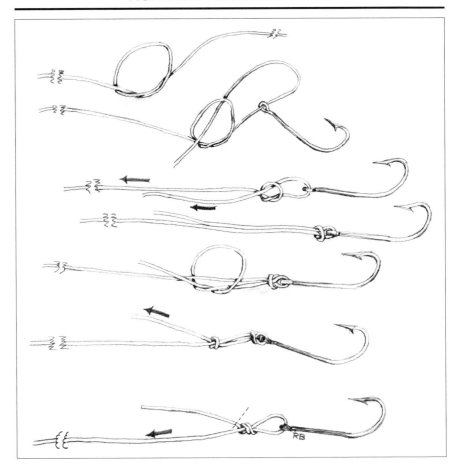

second overhand knot will determine the size of the loop. Finally, pull the tippet so the two overhand knots slide together and pull hard on the short tag end with a pair of pliers to tighten up the knot. Trim the tag end.

Connecting Tippet to Leader, Leader to Fly Line, and Fly Line to Backing

SURGEON'S LOOP KNOT

This is a strong knot that allows quick loop-to-loop connections for ease in replacing tippets, for changing flies with tippet attached, for attaching your leader to your fly line, and for attaching your fly line to your backing. It's very versatile and a snap to tie.

SURGEON'S LOOP KNOT

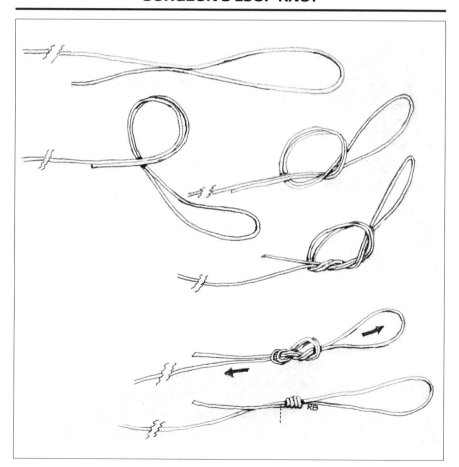

HOW TO TIE First, take the end of the line and fold it over on itself so you have a double line that's about 3 or 4 inches in length. Then take the doubled line and simply tie a double overhand knot. This is done by making the first overhand knot and then wrapping the end over around and through again. To complete the knot, grab the loop in one hand and grab the tag end and line in the other, then gradually pull them apart until tight. Trim the tag end.

Connecting Two Sections of Line

SURGEON'S KNOT

Not to be confused with the surgeon's loop knot, the surgeon's knot is another great knot used in connecting two sections of line, especially of two different diameters as for a tapered leader.

HOW TO TIE Start by taking two sections of line and overlap them by 4 to 6 inches. Use 6 inches if your fingers aren't that nimble: You'll find it easier to tie with a larger loop. Next, while holding the overlapping ends together on the right and left sides separately in your right and left hands, rotate your right hand slightly counterclockwise to form a loop in the double line. Then take the doubled line and simply tie a double overhand knot. This is done by making the first overhand knot and then wrapping the end over around and through again. To complete the knot, grab the left line and tag end in one hand and grab the right line and tag end in the other hand then gradually pull them apart until tight. Trim the tag ends.

BLOOD KNOT

This is another very practical knot for use in connecting two sections of line. The resulting knot will have a straighter connection than the surgeon's knot.

HOW TO TIE Start by taking two sections of line and overlap them by 4 to 6 inches. Then pinch one of the lines and tag ends together on either the left or right side, and with your other hand make eight loose wraps around the line with the other tag end. Insert the tag end in the middle of the wraps and then insert the other tag end through the same opening, but in the opposite direction to increase knot strength. To complete the knot, gradually pull both single lines—*not* the tag ends—until tight. Trim the tag ends. Use more wraps for lighter lines and fewer wraps when tying heavier lines.

SURGEON'S KNOT

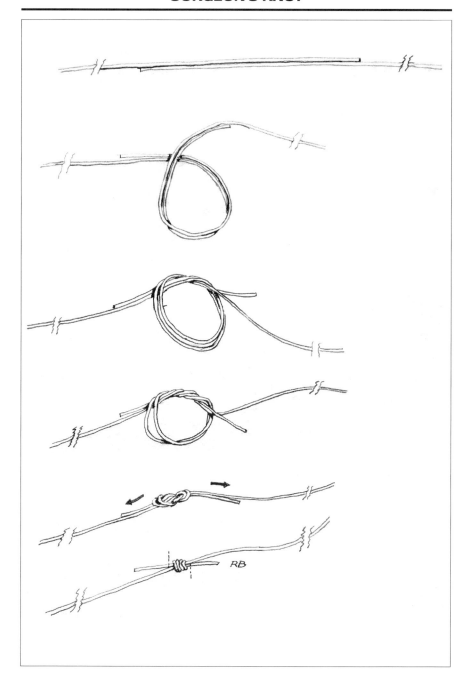

RB

BLOOD KNOT

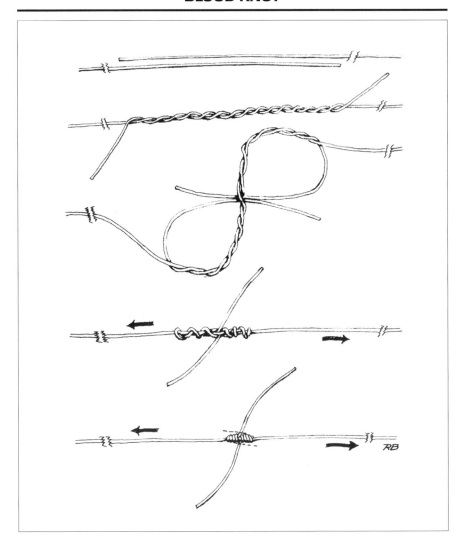

Connecting Leader to Fly Line via Loop-to-Loop

WHIPPED LOOP

Way back when I was just a teenager, I was taught to whip loops on either end of my fly lines for easy loop-to-loop connections. I guess I was taught right, since this is also Lefty's preferred method for connecting the butt section of the leader to the end of the fly line. I've been using it for over 30

WHIPPED LOOP

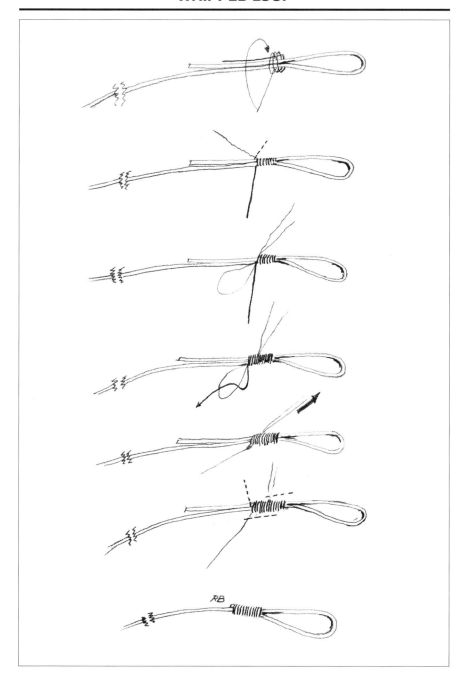

years fishing fresh and salt water, and it has never failed me in all those years. Besides being very reliable and easy to tie, the whipped loop allows for quick and easy loop-to-loop connections.

HOW TO TIE Start by snipping the end of the fly line at an angle so it will be tapered. Next, fold the tip of the line over so it overlaps by about ⅝ to ¾ inch and forms a small loop. Take a bobbin loaded with mono cord or Kevlar that can be pulled fairly tight without breaking. Wrap the thread three or four times around one of the bobbin legs to provide sufficient tension. Then start your thread with a few wraps and hold the line and thread in place between your hands. Now spin the bobbin hard by moving your hands around in a tight circle. The bobbin will begin swinging around, and as it does so it will bury into the fly-line coating and lay down a pattern of thread. By keeping the bobbin swinging and gently raising your right or left hand on a slight angle you can direct the line and move it back and forth across to form a tight and smooth covering of thread. As an alternate method, you can simply put the loop in a fly-tying vise and tie it off. Whip finish or complete the whipped loop by finishing it off as you would when winding a rod guide. Coat the threaded connection with Pliobond, epoxy, or Zap-A-Gap gap-filling formula to make a smooth, durable coating that will slip through the guides easily.

Connecting Fly Line to Backing via Loop-to-Loop

WHIPPED LOOP AND SURGEON'S LOOP

The easiest method the connect the fly line to the backing is via a loop-to-loop connection that will enable you to change fly lines without have to cut and retie your backing connection. This is accomplished by whipping a loop (see above) in the end of your fly line and tying a surgeon's loop knot at the end of your backing (see above). The only difference is that you double the backing over on itself and tie a large 6- to 8-inch surgeon's loop knot on the end of your backing so that it will be large enough to accommodate slipping a large reel through the loop. Make sure you put a small drop of cyanoacrylate on the surgeon's knot for the backing to increase strength. To connect another fly line, just pinch the front portion of the backing loop closed and slide it through the whipped loop of the fly line. Then pull the entire backing loop around your reel. Complete the connection by simply pulling the backing line and loop back through until the loop-to-loop connection is made. Reel the other fly line on and you're all set to go.

CONNECTING FLY LINE TO BACKING

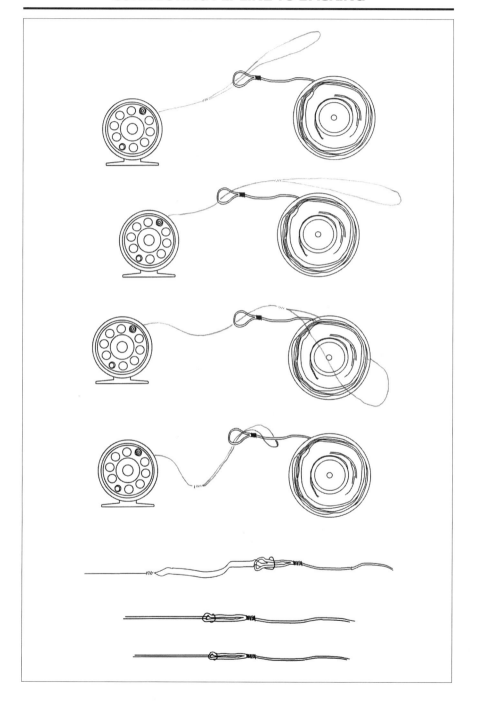

Connecting Backing to Reel

Again, an overhand knot is all that's needed. Start by wrapping the end of the backing around the reel's arbor and then tie an overhand knot around the line. Next, tie an overhand knot or two at the very end of the short tag-end portion of the backing. Essentially, you have made a simple slip knot. Complete the knot by pulling the line tight until snug against the arbor. Then just reel on the backing.

CONNECTING BACKING TO REEL

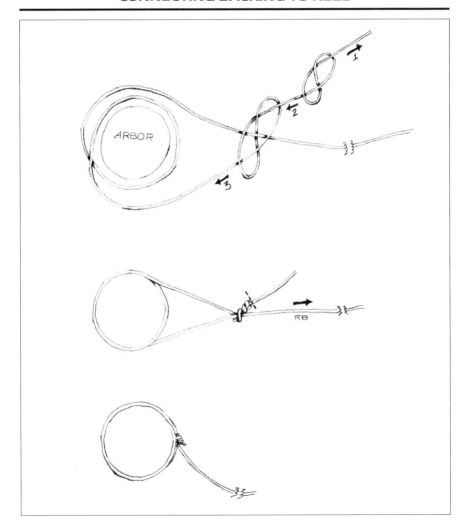

TIPPETS

Whether you're using a straight tippet or a shock tippet, it's important to remember that tippets can and often will take quite a bit of abuse. Tippets can get cut or abraded from coming in contact with structure (rocks, bridge abutments, pilings), tough toothy critters like barracuda and bluefish, and fish with rough abrasive mouths like tarpon, snook, and even large stripers. When rigging up you must consider the fish you will be targeting and rig accordingly. If your target species are toothy, a wire tippet is warranted. I prefer using stainless-steel braided wire. It's easy to tie knots with, hardly kinks, and takes a pretty good beating. Straight wire will usually kink, and your fly will not ride right and will get refused. Bluefish can often be finicky and shy away from wire leaders. In these situations, try using flies tied on longer-shank hooks and heavy 30- to 40-pound mono tippets. Better to lose a few fish than not get any hook-ups.

When fishing for species with tough abrasive mouths, you'll need to use heavier mono tippets. For larger specimens, you'll need to go with a true mono shock leader of 40 to 100 pounds. It sounds incredible, but the abrasive mouth of giant tarpon can saw through even 100-pound mono. Baby tarpon in the 20- to 40-pound range, large snook, and even big stripers will also do a good job chewing up tippets. This is why it's so important to routinely check your tippets for nicks and abrasions. Simply run your fingertips and nail along the tippet's length. If it's chewed up or nicked you should be able to feel the roughness. Mono will quickly lose its strength and will be more likely to break under pressure if there's a nick in the line.

If you fish frequently around structure with sinking lines, your tippets will also develop nicks and abrasions as the line scrapes along the bottom shells, edges of riprap, rock jetties, wrecks, bridge abutments, and so on. Often, your quarry will be hugging these structures and if you don't get that fly right in there nice and tight, you may not get hooked up. If you're not losing a fly on occasion in these locations, you probably aren't fishing it hard enough.

Fish your fly closer, but check your tippet frequently for damage and change it if necessary. In these fishing scenarios, this is extra important because if you do get hooked up it could be with a large fish like a striper or snook. These big, powerful fish will head right back to their homes within the structure and attempt to break you off. You'll need to put maximum pressure on them immediately. That pressure will test your tippet's integrity. If it's damaged, you may have just lost a trophy. Better safe than sorry.

RODS AND REELS

Your rod and reel are vital tools for fighting and subduing your quarry. They ought to match the species and size of fish you are targeting. This is to ensure that you'll be able to apply sufficient pressure on a fish to land and release it in a reasonable amount of time so that it may fight again someday. Reels should have a sufficient line capacity and drag system to accomplish this. For some of the large and/or fast saltwater species like tarpon, big bonefish, permit, big snook and stripers, jacks, and false albacore, large wide-arbor reels with a large reliable disk-drag system and backing capacity of 250 to 300 yards are recommended. Heavier rods in the 9- to 12-weight class with stiffer butt sections for lifting are required. For smaller or slower species like baby tarpon, medium-sized bonefish, redfish, snook, schoolie stripers, sea trout, and ladyfish, lighter 6- to 8-weight rods and reels with a backing capacity of 150 to 250 yards are satisfactory. A 10-weight outfit is ideal for most surf fishing.

A few years ago I was fishing for stripers with a friend who noticed the reel I was using on my 7-weight rod. He asked me how I liked it and I told him it was a great little reel. It had sufficient line capacity and drag for a lot of the saltwater species I often target such as medium-sized snook, redfish, ladyfish, sea trout, and schoolie stripers—like what we were fishing for this day. I was surprised when he told me that he didn't like the reel, because a friend of his got spooled by an albie down at Cape Lookout, North Carolina, and lost everything down to the backing while using the same reel. I had two responses for my friend. First, this *is* a great little reel, but it was not designed with a large-capacity spool or large disk drag to handle the awesome power of false albacore. Second, the angler should have broken the fish off long before he got spooled.

There is a lesson here: Always research and match your equipment to the size and species of fish you plan to target. You should do this for three reasons. First, you want to fight fish fairly. By this I mean enjoy a good pull but be able to land and release fish without them being exhausted and near death. Remember, just because a fish is revived and swims away, it does not necessarily mean that it will live. Many fish that are fought to or near exhaustion will die within hours or a few days. Gamefish are just too valuable to catch only once. Most anglers and especially fly rodders realize this and practice fair fighting and catch-and-release. Here's a saying to remember: *Don't be mean . . . release them when they're green.*

Second, equipment matched to the size and species will maximize your enjoyment of the fight. Many anglers never come close to putting maximum pressure on our awesome saltwater gamesters. I have seen many anglers fight saltwater species with the rod tip like trout on a size 22 and a dainty leader. These are strong, hardy fish! My good friend's wife Carol Mentzer is a terrific fly fisher. When she fishes with her husband Greg for stripers and false albacore, she sticks it to them good. She understands exactly how to fight these fish by really leaning on them with a lot of side pressure. She knows she's not going to pull the lips off the fish. These are really tough fish, and anglers need to fight them hard. Albies are typically fought on 10-weight rods with large-arbor reels with a minimum of 250 yards of backing, a large disk-drag system, and a 12- to 20-pound tippet. Carol does everything right: She pulls hard, has a fair fight, gets the fish in as quickly as possible while still pretty green, and does a quick release so her fish can fight again. She can do this because she has the properly matched rod and reel and she knows how to put maximum pressure on fish.

On the other hand, using a 10-weight outfit on schoolie stripers, sea trout, ladyfish, or bluefish in the 2- to 6-pound range is being too heavy-handed. Anglers using such equipment are missing out on a lot of fun. By moving down to a 6- or 7-weight outfit, you can maximize the pull while still being able to bring the fish in quickly and release them green.

Finally, if your outfit is properly matched, you'll be able to catch and release more fish when the fishing gets hot than someone using a lighter outfit who has to fight the fish much longer to tire them out before bringing them in. As mentioned, this is dangerous to the fish.

HOOKING UP—WHEN AND HOW TO STRIKE

There are some big differences between fishing in fresh water and fishing in salt. Saltwater fish are generally much larger, stronger, and faster. Their mouths are tougher, and hooks are larger and more difficult to drive in for a good, solid hookset. Tarpon have mouths as large and tough as a metal bucket. The gentle, dainty raising-the-rod-tip hookset needed for some trout-fishing situations just won't cut it for these tough saltwater critters. Another factor that many converted freshwater fishermen fail to account for is the longer casts and greater length of line that must be pulled tight before a hook can be set properly. Improper hook setting is a very common flaw for saltwater fly-fishing novices. I often hear anglers new to the salt explaining that they got hooked up, but the fish just popped off. Most of those fish didn't just pop off; for many the hook was never set correctly to begin with and easily worked loose. Unfortunately, many of these anglers never realize what's happening and therefore never change their strategies for ensuring a more solid hookset. The good news is, it can be easily corrected if you practice the following.

Strip-Striking with a One-Handed Retrieve

Strip-striking is by far the most effective method for setting a hook in saltwater species. These are tough fish. Don't worry, properly setting a hook hard with a strip-strike will not cause serious injury to the fish and won't break your rod. The strip-strike is actually a natural follow-through when retrieving your fly. A common mistake made by many saltwater anglers, especially new folks, is that they retrieve the fly with their rods held well above the water and up in the air. This creates a lot of slack in the line, which must be removed before you can even think about setting the hook. It also puts the rod in an awkward and incorrect position to perform the strip-strike.

The rod tip should be kept pointing down low to the water. This minimizes slack and puts the angler in the right position to make a strip-strike. Greg and Carol Mentzer demonstrate how it's done while fish structure in and around the Chesapeake Bay Bridge.

While retrieving your fly, keep your rod pointed down, just above or even slightly below the surface of the water and straight at your fly. This will keep your fly line straight, and you'll be able to feel a strike when a fish takes your fly. The instant a strike is detected, perform a strip-strike by sharply pulling or stripping the line down and away to the side while at the same time pulling your rod hand sharply back and away in the opposite direction. One or two strip-strikes is usually all you need to set the hook firmly. With the fly line being pulled sharply in one direction and the rod butt being pulled back in the opposite direction, slack is removed and the line comes tight, setting the hook firmly in the fish's mouth. If you miss the fish or the fly pulls loose, keep on stripping. Repeat the process if the fly is taken again.

The strip-strike is performed in conjunction with and as a continuation of your regular retrieve of the fly. With your line straight and rod tip pointed down, continue to strip in your fly or follow your fly on the swing or dead drift. When you feel a fish take your fly as either a hard strike, a gentle bump, or a gulp on the surface, immediately perform the strip-strike. It's important to only perform the strip-strike when you feel resis-

A bluefish smashes a fly just a few feet from the end of the rod. Many gamefish will follow a fly back and won't strike until within just a few feet of your position, whether in a boat or in the surf. Be prepared for these exciting strikes by keeping your rod tip pointed down, maintaining a tight line, keeping alert, and retrieving the fly all the way back.

tance or something unusual. Sometimes it may be nothing but a piece of weed or a clamshell, but many times fish will take the fly surprisingly softly. All you may feel is a slight tap or bump that may indicate the fish has sucked in your fly.

To perform the strip-strike properly, there are a several other things to keep in mind. First, while you are pulling the rod butt back and to the side, you should still keep the rod tip pointed straight at your fly and fish. Avoid the bad habit of raising your rod tip upward right away, as when fishing for trout. As soon as you do that, you decrease the amount of pressure on the hook point and will often fail to set it firmly in place. With the rod tip pointed up at the eleven to twelve o'clock position and sharply bent downward, there is actually very little pressure being placed on the hook or the fish. When you strip-strike and pull back with the rod at a slight angle, maximum pressure is being applied. You should feel the butt of the rod bending slightly while the tip of the rod remains relatively straight. During the strip strike, remember to keep the fly line tight against the rod handle. Don't let it slip. This will reduce tension and pressure. For extra insurance, pull the fly line and pump the rod to the side a few more times to ensure a solid hookset. For tarpon, you'll need to do this as many times as you can before the fish jumps. After the initial strip-strike, add a few extra pumps with the rod to the side. You should be hooked solidly and can lift your rod, because the fish will usually run hard or surge.

Strip-Striking with a Two-Handed Retrieve

The difference here is that you have the rod handle tucked up under the crux of your armpit. This frees both hands for retrieving. With the two-handed retrieve, you will need to strip-strike sharply several times with either hand to ensure a solid hookset. Once the fish is on, you just need to maintain line pressure and reposition the rod for fighting.

The Short Strip-Strike

I use what I call a short strip-strike when sight fishing the shallows for bottom feeders including bonefish and redfish. The rationale for using a short strip-strike was discussed in strategy 5, under "Don't Yank the Fly Away." Essentially, the shortened strip-strike is used to prevent making a long strip that could pull the fly out of the fish's strike zone in the event the fish has not taken the fly or the fly slips out of the fish's mouth. Sight fishing

For a two-handed retrieve, hold the rod under your arm and alternate hands to retrieve and provide lifelike motion to the fly. Upon detecting a strike, simply pull sharply with either or both hands and maintain a tight line. Once the fish is on, reposition the rod for fighting. The use of a stripping basket will help control loose line.

often involves far fewer encounters with fish, so it's wise to make each one count.

When a bonefish or redfish appears to have taken the fly, I pull my elbows and forearms tight into my sides and bring my hands close together in order to greatly reduce their movement. I then like to run a test by giving one or two very slight short tugs of just 1 or 2 inches on the line to see if the fish has the fly. If it doesn't, there won't be any resistance. If there's resistance, a fish has the fly, in which case I'll give two or three sharp, rapid, but very short 4- to 6-inch strip-strikes. Bonefish and redfish have soft rubbery lips. A few short, sharp, rapid strip-strikes will easily make for a solid hookset, after which the rod can be raised to fight the fish. In the event that the fish doesn't have the fly or it slipped out of the fish's mouth, the short strip-strike will pull the fly a short distance away, but still within the strike zone. Usually, the fish thinks the fly escaped and will aggressively attack it. A long strip-strike and raised rod in these situations would pull the fly outside the fish's strike zone, and you'd have lost an opportunity.

FIGHTING AND LANDING FISH

To land a fish you must stay connected. The key to staying connected is in controlling the line while maintaining tension on the fish. With few exceptions, tight lines are where it's at. For the saltwater neophyte, this is easier said than done. I was one, I know. Once a fish is hooked, there are three ways to control the line and maintain pressure: with your hands, with the reel, and with the rod.

Controlling the Line

Being able to control your line using your hands while fighting a fish from beginning to end is a key skill that you'll need to master if you wish to be more successful. First, you'll need to control the line with your rod hand. This is accomplished by maintaining the line between your fingers and the rod handle until all the slack is on the reel. During the initial strip-strike, your fingers should be just loosely holding the line so you can pull down sharply with your nonrod hand. This next step is very important. Once you've strip-striked and the fish is on, immediately squeeze down with your rod hand's index finger to apply pressure to the line so that it will not slip or be pulled easily. This is important because it will keep your line tight to the fish while you release the line in your nonrod hand to regrab hold of the line immediately behind as it exits your rod hand. If the fish is strong and pulls hard, ease up a bit on your rod hand and let the fish pull some line. With your nonrod hand, you can now once again strip line in to maintain pressure on the fish as necessary. Always maintain control of and pressure on the line with your rod hand, and always pull line in with your nonrod hand. By doing it this way, your nonrod hand will always know it can grab the line immediately behind your rod hand. You don't have to look for it . . . you can simply feel for it. Many anglers make the mistake of letting go of the line with the rod hand and lose concentration because they have to look for the line to grab. Often slack will develop in the line, and the fish will come off.

Stripping in several fish during the course of the day usually won't cause wear and tear on your hands or your finger joints. However, when you anticipate blind casting hundreds of times and catching numerous fish, I strongly advise wearing fighting gloves that will protect your fingers. These gloves cover only the first and second fingers, except for the very tips, to permit freedom of motion and dexterity. With your first and second fingers protected from injury due to line friction, you'll be able to comfortably retrieve line all day and place significant pressure on the line during a fight from your rod hand and/or line hand without pain and without bleeding all over your equipment, clothes, and clean deck.

Once hooked, many species of fish such as stripers, sea trout, redfish, and bluefish will shake their heads and make a few quick lunges in an attempt to get away or get loose. Anglers often misinterpret this, thinking that the fish is making a run; they let go of the line, losing control. Often, the fish pulls out several feet of line and stops to do some more head shaking and thrashing. Unfortunately, this usually puts slack in the line, and the fish pops off. Don't be fooled by this tactic. Maintain line control and pressure. If the fish is going to run, let it pull the line from your hands. Loosen your grip a bit so the line can slide out under slight pressure. If the fish stops, simply apply pressure with your rod hand.

A critical point for many anglers comes when they must decide whether or not to put the fish on the reel. Once hooked, fast species that often make long runs like bonefish, albies, permit, and tarpon will usually make that decision for you very quickly. However, many other species like stripers, bluefish, redfish, and snook have more of a bulldog style of fighting, with a few short runs in between to make things interesting, but often not long enough to clear all your line from the deck and get on the reel. My recommendation is to only put fish on the reel if they earn it. I see all too many saltwater anglers lose fish because while they were worrying about reeling in loose line, they lost concentration, slack developed, and the fish popped off. Avoid this by simply stripping the fish in by hand while maintaining control of and pressure on the line. Slip line out if the fish surges, and then quickly retrieve line again by stripping. During a good year, I'll often catch and release many striped bass, yet I will only use the reel only about 10 percent of the time. Most of these stripers are simply stripped in by hand without use of the reel. Yes, many are smaller schoolie-sized fish in the 3- to 10-pound range that one would expect to strip in, but many of these also include fish in the 15- to 30-pound range. Some of the hotter stripers I find are those in the midteens. These teenagers have an attitude, want to burn some line, and often get on the reel, while some of the bigger fish just dog it, staying close by. Redfish can almost always be counted on to peel off some line during a fight. Usually when first hooked they will bolt with several 20- to 30-yard surges. Sometimes that's enough to earn the reel. Other times, they'll make a short run and then settle down and bull-

Once a fish is hooked solid, raise the rod and maintain control of the line so it remains tight. If the fish is not taking line, you should be retrieving line. (Photo: Greg and Carol Mentzer)

dog you good. This is when you'll need to be concerned with maintaining line control and a tight line with your hands by continuing to strip in line as the fish gets closer. When first hooked, snook will immediately try to get back to the cover of the mangroves or a structure like a bridge. You must maintain very strict line control by keeping a tight line and stripping in line as quickly as possible to prevent the snook from getting back to its lair and breaking the leader. There is no time to even think about getting the fish on the reel until the fish is pulled well clear of any mangroves or structure.

Fighting on the Reel

As mentioned above, my recommendation is to put fish on the reel only if they earn it. Fast species like bonefish, permit, tarpon, false albacore, bonito, and barracuda will earn the right to be on your reel in about as much time as it takes to say . . . *yee-hah!* Immediately after the hook is set, these lightning-fast fish usually take off on a least one or two blistering runs. This is definitely not the time to be trying to determine the proper setting of your reel's drag pressure. You should always preset your reel's drag pressure prior to fishing. As I've gained more on-the-water experience,

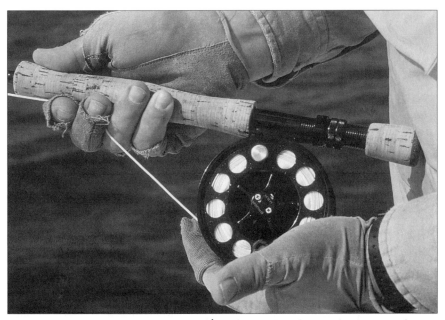

Squeeze line against the rod handle and/or palm the rim of the reel to increase drag as needed. Fighting gloves on hard-fighting fish will reduce cuts and abrasions from the line.

I've moved away from setting my reels with heavy drag pressure. I hear many anglers claim that their reel has a drag that can stop a freight train. The simple fact of the matter is that your reel's drag pressure should be set at only at about 2-3 pounds of pressure. That's it! It is far more important that your reel have a nice smooth drag, not a heavy one.

Years ago when fishing for big bonefish (8 to 10 pounds) and false al-bacore (12 to 16 pounds), I began experimenting with my drag pressure. I would crank down on the drag with 12 to 14 pounds of pressure in an attempt to keep their blistering runs short and more manageable. Amazingly, these incredibly powerful fish would rise to the challenge and still peel off 100 or 150 yards and more of line. I think they actually got pissed off and fought even harder. The other problem was that fish would often break the tippet when transitioning from one surge to the next. Apparently slack would develop, and with a heavy drag the line was not re-leased gradually enough and would just snap. This is similar to taking an 8-pound section of mono and pulling it gradually between your two hands. It's difficult to break. Instead take the same line, put 6 to 8 inches of slack in it, then pull your hands apart quickly. The line breaks easily under the sudden stress. I then experimented by resetting the drag pressure down to only about 3 pounds. What I found was that the fish usually didn't run nearly as far with the lighter drag setting, plus I wouldn't break a tippet if they surged. Once the long initial runs were over, I could use my fingers to adjust and provide maximum pressure as needed to pump the fish in.

Your first priority in fighting a fish on the reel is to clear the line on the deck and get the line on the reel. To accomplish this you need to form an "okay" sign around the line with your line hand after the strip-strike and only after the fish starts its run. The "okay" sign will act as a large guide to help clear any tangles and control excess line between your reel and the first stripping guide so that it will go through the rod guides smoothly without any hang-ups. If the fish slows down its run, gently close down the "okay" sign formed by your line hand and put some pressure on the line to prevent slack from forming and to maintain a tight line. The more line you have on the boat deck, in your stripping basket, or trailing behind you, the greater the chance that it may get knotted and/or tangled as it rapidly gets pulled by the fish. When fish follow and take the fly right at the boat or your feet, there can often be 50 to 80 feet of line that may need to be cleared.

After the fish has begun its run and you have formed the "okay" sign, you'll need to focus all your attention on making sure all your line clears and gets on the reel. You should not be looking at where the fish is going or the expression on your buddy's face. You should be watching your line to make sure you're not standing on it, that it's not wrapped around your leg, that it hasn't caught on the reel butt or around something in the boat, and that there are no tangles. If there are, you have to move fast to clear or untangle the line before the fish comes tight. Otherwise your leader will likely snap and you will have lost the fish. Often there is no time to untie a tangled line. If the tangle is quite large or looks like a bird's nest and you doubt that it will fit through the guides, you have but one choice: You'll have to grab the line and pop the fish off to prevent damage to the guides. On the other hand, there is a trick for getting smaller tangles through the guides without hanging up. If you're clearing line and you notice a small knot or tangle, point the rod at the fish and simply rotate the rod over so the reel and guides are pointing up. The knot or tangle should slip through. If you manage to stay connected to the fish, just repeat the process and reel the knot or tangle onto the reel, untying it after you land the fish.

Many anglers fail to properly clear and control their line during these critical times. They're often too busy hooting and hollering and never look down to see that they're standing on the line. When the fish starts screaming out line, it has a tendency to jump around a bit and will catch on the oddest things. On my first false albacore trip down at Cape Lookout, North Carolina, I hooked up with an albie that started ripping out line. I had fished for bonefish for years so this was nothing unusual. As the line was quickly flying off the deck, it jumped and managed to wrap itself around the exposed tips of my fly rods that were stored horizontally under the gunwale. The boat I was fishing in had a rod storage configuration that did not feature rod tip protectors. Although I'd done this hundreds of times before, I did exactly what I was supposed to do and watched my line clear. It didn't and got wrapped around the rod tips, so I simply squeezed and held the line tight. When the albie reached the end of its line it popped the 16-pound tippet like a light thread. I lost a fish, but I could have broken two rods and limited my fishing. In situations where there is a small amount of line that has not been cleared and can be easily and quickly wound back on the reel, I'll often do it. Just remember to maintain hand pressure on the fish until you're on the reel.

Once the fish is on the reel, you can let it run or apply additional drag pressure by palming the exposed rim of the reel to create friction. When palming or applying hand pressure to the exposed reel rim, remember to do so gradually. If you suddenly apply too much pressure and cause the release of line to jerk, you run the risk of snapping your tippet and losing the fish. With direct-drive reels you'll need to exercise caution to avoid getting your knuckles whacked. You'll also need to develop a "feel" when reeling in line to know when the fish is beginning to run or surge so you can remove your hand from the spinning handle. After you get you knuckles banged up a few times, you'll quickly learn to feel it coming.

A basic rule to remember when fighting fish is that either the fish should be taking line or you should be putting line on the reel. If not, the fish is resting and gaining strength. This will prolong the fight, increasing the risk of losing and/or killing the fish. After their initial runs, many fish will double back and swim toward you. When this happens you'll often lose touch with the fish. It may feel as if the fish has come loose. When this happens you must rapidly retrieve slack line to get back in touch with and maintain pressure on the fish. The new large-arbor reels have the ability to retrieve line at a much higher rate and are thus very desirable for species that make long runs. Standard-arbor reels are still perfectly fine for most fishing situations—you just have to reel a little faster and longer.

In some special circumstances, it may be best to actually back off and not use any drag—sharks chasing hooked bonefish immediately comes to mind. Small sharks are almost always present when you fish the flats for bonefish. Often during the course of a day, you may encounter a shark chasing a bonefish you just hooked. They're attracted to the frantic behavior of the hooked fish and think it's injured and an easy meal. You have a few choices: Let the shark chomp your bonefish; point your rod at the fish, reel in tight, and pop it off to fight another day; or release the drag, let the bonefish run free of the shark, then reel it back in. With a very light drag, a bonefish will still be able to outrun most sharks. If it doesn't, pop it off to save it and possibly you from a "close encounter" of a toothy kind.

Backing off on your drag can also sometimes prevent you from getting cut off and losing a fish. A few years back, I was bonefishing in the Turks and Caicos Islands. It was my last day and my last shot at a bonefish before heading back. We just finished poling across the last flat and started entering some deeper water along a mangrove edge. Arthur Dean, my guide and the owner-operator of Silver Deep Charters, told me to stay on the bow a little while longer. He said that some big bones sometimes hang on the edge of this deeper water. Sure enough, a short distance away I spotted a large dark shape swimming the edge in about 4 feet of water. It was a 10-pound bone. I made the cast, let the fly sink down, and gave it a few short strips before coming tight. The large bone felt the hook and took off like a silver rocket along the mangrove edge. I knew I was flirting with danger with the mangroves so close, but I wasn't expecting its next move. After a hair-raising run the bone made a sharp right-hand turn at the end of the mangroves, which went into a small bay. I had only one choice. I immediately cut all the way back on the drag and gave the fish slack. The line stopped suddenly. I hoped for the best and began reeling in line as Arthur poled the boat to where the line led. As we rounded the corner we found that the bone had gone only under several mangrove roots on the outer edge. I hung myself over the bow and worked the entire rod and reel under the mangroves. After reeling in the slack line, I soon found myself tight once again to the bonefish. It was just sitting there trying to figure the whole thing out. I think it was as surprised as we were. A short time later I was fortunate to land the beautiful 10-pounder.

Once fish have completed their long runs, they settle down and slug it out. However, with saltwater fish you won't be able to simply reel the fish in. They are too strong. As I describe below under "Fighting with the Rod," you must pump the rod and then reel to gain line. Saltwater fish will peel off much more line than freshwater fish. It is very important that you use your fingers to guide the backing and fly line back on your reel spool so that it stays level and does not stack up on one side or the other. Line that stacks on one side of the spool will often collapse and cause the line to jam. I use the pinkie of my reel hand to perform this important task. Periodically I'll look down as I'm reeling in line to make sure it is going on level. If you run your backing clear across the spool and back again occasionally while you're retrieving line, it will prevent your backing from digging in and possibly jamming.

Fighting with the Rod

Believe me, you won't be waltzing saltwater fish around on light tippets with the bulk of the fight taking place in the upper 2 or 3 feet of your rod tip. For the majority of saltwater fish, you'll need to put on some serious pressure and fight using the butt section of the rod. Many anglers new to the salt think that the more the rod is bent, the more pressure is exerted. This is simply not true. When a rod is maintained in a near-vertical position with the upper third of the rod tip severely bent over, there is actually very little pressure being exerted—perhaps only 2 or 3 pounds. To effectively fight saltwater fish you must point the rod at the fish in a near-horizontal position and then apply side pressure until the rod is bent at a maximum angle of about 45 degrees. In this position the rod's thicker butt section can be effectively used to exert maximum pressure while only causing the rod tip to bend slightly. There are instances when it is desirable for you to change this tactic. For instance, during the initial run and during the fight when a fish surges, your rod should be pointed directly at the fish or slightly vertical to minimize pressure. Also, holding the rod high during these runs is desirable when fishing the flats to avoid rubbing or entangling the line along the bottom or against sharp coral, sea fans, or mangrove shoots. When the fish settles down, maximum side pressure should again be applied to subdue it.

Rick Bender is being tested by a big, tough offshore albie. It's important to maintain maximum pressure by keeping the rod low at a 45-degree angle. Notice how Rick is letting the fish pull the rod down in the water but is keeping the rod clear of the gunwale. With that amount of pressure, the rod will shatter if it touches the gunwale.

Direction of pressure is also essential. By holding the rod low and to the opposite side of where the fish is heading, maximum leverage can be applied. If the fish is swimming out and away to the left, you should be pulling back to the right. If the fish changes direction and begins pulling away to the right, you should change rod position and be pulling back to the left and so on. Maintaining low side pressure is the key to subduing fish quickly. With low side pressure, fish are kept off balance.

Larger and stronger fish can often get very stubborn and hunker down, not wanting to budge. This can happen when you're fishing from shore or from a boat. If steady pressure fails to move the fish, try pumping the rod up and down several times with a few short bursts as if you were setting the hook while you also change the angle of pressure. Usually this tactic is enough to force the fish to move toward you and/or away from its holding position.

To retrieve line you'll need to pump the fish in using the lifting strength of the rod's butt section. Simply hold the end of the rod butt firmly against your stomach, pinch the line against the rod handle to maximize the pressure, and pull back, slightly upward, and to the side with the rod handle until the rod is bent in a 45-degree angle. Then, while maintaining slight tension, let the rod drop down toward the fish while reeling simultaneously. Lower the rod gradually, but never faster than you can reel in the line. You don't want any slack to develop. If it does, you could lose the fish. Keep repeating this process to gain line on the reel. If while you're pumping the rod back you feel the fish surge or shake its head, relieve your finger pressure to give the fish a little line—but only if needed. Before you give line, a fish should earn it. If you feel it trying to surge, make it bend the rod first before giving line. Often stripers, redfish, and albies will pump their tails near the end of the fight, but they usually don't have enough juice left to really take off. They pull a little harder and bend the rod a little farther, which produces a little more pressure. Usually the rod goes up and down a few times, but the fish cannot sustain the effort and the rod begins to straighten. Then you can reel down and retrieve more line.

Fighting a fish from the beach or from a boat in shallow water is quite a bit easier then fighting one in deep water, since the fish is essentially being pulled or slid in from the side toward you. Fighting fish in deep water is quite different in that the fight entails not only pulling the fish in from the side, but also lifting it up through the water column. Lifting a fish is tougher. Pulling it through and against the water column adds a considerable amount of resistance and makes the final episode of the battle much more difficult. I think this is why some anglers feel that false albacore fight much harder than bonefish. I think they are pretty close to being equally strong. The difference is due to the water depth. Bonefish are in shallow water so they are more easily pulled or slid sideways through the water toward the angler. Once albies get close to the boat, however, they go deep and are very difficult to pull up against the water, making them seem even tougher than they really are.

When fighting fish like albies, stripers, and jacks in deeper water from a boat, be prepared to lift them up through the water with your rod as opposed to sliding them in from the beach. This takes more patience and care, since these fish seem to instinctively know that staying deep and circling the boat will cause havoc topside. This is especially true fishing each fall in the Cape Lookout area of North Carolina for false albacore. You must be ready to dance around and around the deck of the boat as albies go in circles. One angler is tough enough, but when there's a double hook-up, watch out. You must pay strict attention to where the lines are and must do some orchestrating to keep lines clear. Albies as well as stripers, jacks, and other large fish will also surge under the boat and toward the bottom repeatedly. You need to be ready to move alongside the gunwale, brace yourself with your knees, and lean overboard with the rod to avoid letting the rod touch the top of the gunwale. If a rod touches the top of the gunwale while under pressure, it's almost a guarantee that it will break immediately. Most of the time you must literally shove the entire rod under the water alongside the boat sometimes all the way up to the reel and then waltz around to the other side of the boat. This is especially tough if you have to go around the outboard, but who said it was going to be easy?

Another effective technique to subdue tougher fish is to try to roll them over when they're within 15 feet or so. Rolling a fish over tends to disorient it. To accomplish this, pull the fish to one side or the other. As the fish yields to the pressure and is slid to the side, gradually lift and then pull the rod in the opposite direction, trying to roll the fish over in the process. It doesn't work every time, but with practice you'll have more success. While the fish is disoriented you can apply maximum pressure, recover more line, and slide the fish toward you in preparation for landing.

If you have been fortunate to get your fish within 20 feet or so, you stand an excellent chance of landing it. Still, this is the time when most fish are lost. When fish are close at hand, it's time to be more cautious; be ready to finesse the fish and exert measured pressure. Remember, during a prolonged tough fight your leader and its various connections have been tested to the limit, and your leader and tippet may have sustained abrasions and nicks. Most importantly, remember that you are probably somewhat tired and anxious, and are more likely to try to horse the fish in the last few feet. This is often the moment of truth when cooler heads should prevail. Take your time, be patient, and watch the fish for signs that the battle is over. Many times when fish are brought near the boat for the first time, they may appear ready—but will go ballistic and bolt. Be ready to finesse a fish and give it a little rod to soften its trust. Try not to give it any line unless it earns it. At best, a fish will usually only bend and pump the rod or take a few feet of line. This is a sure sign that the battle is nearly over. If it makes a good run, be patient, apply pressure to wear it down again, and repeat the process. However, the second time to the boat or land, the fish should be ready for landing.

Landing Fish

If you are fishing from the beach or a jetty, use the waves to help bring the fish to shore. Smaller fish can often be safely landed from a jetty by lifting them with the rod or by pulling the line up by hand once they're close to the rocks. Jetties are often quite treacherous with no place to safely reach the water's edge to land a large fish. Rather than risking your safety, maintain control of the fish, but do not bring it in close to the rocks where it can break you off. Instead maintain a tight line by giving or retrieving line as necessary, and carefully work back to the beach where you can safely land the fish. Once the fish is near the breaking waves, maintain steady pressure to hold it in place until the next wave comes. As the wave approaches, apply more rod pressure and walk backward if possible. The key is to apply steady pressure so the fish comes toward shore with the extra help of the wave. You will probably need the help of several waves to beach larger fish, so be patient. Maintain pressure while you wait for the next wave and repeat the process until the fish comes ashore. Try to slide the fish up as far as possible with the help of the wave so that when the wave retreats the fish will be on the beach out of the water. This should give you enough time to hustle down to grab your fish.

When wade fishing or fishing from shore where there are rips or strong currents, gamefish will instinctively use the fast water to help them fight.

Trying to pull them from the current is usually a fruitless effort. You're better off walking carefully downcurrent along the shore to resume the fight. With you pulling the rod downcurrent and the fish trying to swim upcurrent, the fish will tire quickly. If you can, carefully work the fish into slower water where you can safely land it. Spending time and getting to know the area's waters beforehand will tell you not only where to find fish but also where to land them safely.

Landing fish from a boat is a little easier since you'll have firm footing, access to landing tools like nets, Boga Grips, and gaffs, as well as perhaps

Fish without teeth like snook and stripers can be safely landed and released by grabbing or "lipping" their bottom jaw.

the help of a friend. I do almost exclusively catch-and-release fishing these days, so I rarely use a net to land fish; I land almost all of them by hand or with the use of a Boga Grip. I feel that the net will damage the fish's protective slime covering. Besides, if the fish falls out . . . it's just a quick release.

For a quick landing, work your fish within about 10 feet of the boat or your position on the bank and try getting its head above water. As soon as you do this, pinch the line tight against the rod handle, keep the fish's head just above the water, and with steady pressure slide the fish in toward the boat or under the net. To do this, you'll need to gradually bring the rod up to a more vertical position and pull the rod handle back along your side. On various Web sites, anglers often voice their trouble landing fish with a long fly rod, since the fish is so far away from the boat. The trouble is not with the fly rod. Usually the angler has reeled the fish too far in with the rod held in a horizontal position. If you try to lift even a small fish with just the rod tip, you'll risk breaking the rod. Instead, reel the fish only to about 10 feet of the rod tip. As you lift and pull back on your rod toward a more vertical position, the extra line will allow the fish to slide freely right up alongside you or the boat for an easy release. If you happen to have a little too much line out and the fish is still too far away to land, simply rotate the rod handle so that the reel faces away from your back. This will allow you to push your arm and the rod all the way back to slide the fish in to you. With smaller fish, you can even apply pressure with your thumb to push the rod down in a more horizontal position to take up more line.

Once the fish is alongside, you can now land it. Many fish can be safely and easily landed with just your hands. Fish like stripers and small and medium-sized snook that just have slightly abrasive dentures can be lipped using your thumb and index finger. You do have to be careful of their sharp gill plate covers if they thrash around. After landing 20 or 30 stripers you may wind up with a slightly chewed-up thumb. We call it "striper thumb" and wear it proudly for the next few days as a reminder of a great day's fishing. Other fish like bonefish and smaller redfish can be landed by gently placing one hand under their stomach to cradle them while grabbing the base of their tail with the other. If you grab them across the top of their back and gently turn them upside down, you'll notice that they go almost completely limp for easy hook removal.

Fish like false albacore, tuna, Spanish macs, and even bluefish that have narrow tapered tail stems can be easily landed by grabbing the base of the tail. Again, turning the fish upside down will usually calm it down for easy hook removal. The bony tail stems of flapping albies can eventually cause abrasions. A glove that is coated with silicone beads makes landing larger fish even easier. Extreme caution must be used when handling fish with dangerously sharp teeth like barracuda, Spanish/king mackerel, and bluefish. Their teeth are razor sharp. Always use a pair of pliers or specialized hook removers to safely extract hooks from these toothy critters. Also, be especially careful not to clutch these fish against your body while removing the hook or for any other reason. My friend Rick Bender was surf fishing in Delaware and witnessed a horrible incident involving an angler and a large 12-pound bluefish. The angler was having difficulty holding the fish while removing the hook. The fish was slipping out of his hands and rather than let the fish fall, he reacted by clutching the fish against his chest to hold it firmly in place. One thing you must always remember about bluefish: They will bite you and hold on to you if they can. As soon as the fish got close enough to the angler, it lashed out and bit down with a viselike grip right on the man's exposed neck. Blood was spurting everywhere as the angler began to scream in pain. Luckily, Rick and another person were

Using a Boga Grip is an effective way to land and release fish, especially for fish with sharp or pointy teeth, like bluefish and sea trout. (Photo: Greg and Carol Mentzer)

on hand. The one angler held the fish steady while Rick reached inside its gill covers to force its jaw open and free the angler. Luckily for the angler, the wounds were not too deep. As for the bluefish, it wasn't as lucky . . . it was dinner the following night. Bluefish are serious customers and always seem pissed off. Don't give them an opportunity to chomp you—because they will. It's just they way they are.

Large stripers, redfish, snook, bluefish, jacks, and other fish may need to be landed by net or by placing your hand just inside the outer edge of the gill covers and lifting, being especially careful not to touch or cause damage to the fish's sensitive gills. One of the safest and easiest ways to land large and small fish alike is with the use of a Boga Grip. With the Boga Grip strapped around your wrist, all you need to do is pull back on the spring-loaded catch to open the C-shaped grips. Then simply place the Boga Grip on the fish's lower jaw and release the catch. The C-shaped grips close and lock in place, thereby holding the fish. You can then just hold the handle of the Boga Grip to hold and/or revive the fish. At the time of release, just pull back on the spring-loaded catch; the C grips open and the fish swims freely away. No harm, no foul.

A lip gaff is commonly used to land larger fish like tarpon and cobia.

For truly large fish like giant tarpon and cobia, use a lip gaff to land or stabilize the fish while the hook is removed. The gaff is essentially thrust through the lower lip of the fish as if hooked. The lip gaff does minimal damage to large fish, which can in turn be released safely to fight another day.

Reviving and Releasing Fish

Whether it's a schoolie striper or a 10-pound bone fish, there is always a very special moment when I am reviving a healthy fish in preparation for releasing it back into its natural environment. Time seems to stand still. I try to take in and absorb every detail of the fish's color and beauty as it lies suspended in my hands. I think of how fortunate I am to share the moment and remind myself of how important it is for all of us to release these magnificent creatures so that we and our children may share more magical moments in the future.

As mentioned earlier in this strategy, the key to releasing fish in good shape with a high potential for survival is ensuring that you use an adequately matched rod and reel and that you apply sufficient pressure to land the fish quickly while they're still green. Fish landed relatively quickly should still have quite a bit of fight in them. If you play a fish until there's no fight left, you have essentially exhausted it, and it will probably die as a consequence.

A great way to release fresh fish is to simply remove the hook, if possible without actually touching them, while they are still in the water. If you can't remove the hook by hand, a stainless-steel needle-nose pliers can be used if the hook is accessible. However, if a fish has fought hard and appears to be fatigued, hold it right side up in the water until it begins to show signs of movement or simply flicks its tail and bolts away. Striped bass and snook can be held by their lower jaw in the water. When they're ready to go, they usually clamp down on your fingers to let you know. If you don't get out of the way, you may wind up with a face full of water as a good-bye.

Obviously, you don't want to lip any fish that have teeth like bluefish, sea trout, kingfish, 'cuda, and the like. You can cradle these fish, keeping your hands well away from the toothy end, or hold them by the tail, giving them a few pushes back and forth to get the water circulating. For fish like false albacore that can be grabbed and held by the tail, just remove the hook, hold the fish at chest height, and launch the albie straight down into the water like a big fat lawn dart. The rush of water over their gills usually charges their battery very quickly, and they swim off.

Taking pictures of fish while out of the water can lead to excess mortality if it is not done correctly. First, avoid taking the fish out of the water. The fish's oxygen level is already depleted. If the fish is removed from the water, its oxygen level will drop even lower. This would be like if you just finished a marathon and someone held you under water for a few minutes to take a few pictures. Can you imagine how you would feel gasping for oxygen? Well, the fish you catch probably feel pretty much the same way. So when you catch a fish, leave it in the water to let it catch its breath, so to speak. If you have a friend with you, this would be a good time to get the camera ready. When he is set, lift up the fish and take a few shots. If you need a few more, put the fish back in the water and repeat the process. Then make sure you take extra time if needed to revive the fish. I use this technique routinely and can say from experience that if you have fought the fish fairly, gotten it to the boat quickly, and kept it in the water while preparing for pictures, the fish should be green and good to go when you release it.

Our gamefish are too important a resource to be caught just once. Take the time to revive fish and safely release them so we may enjoy the magic another day.

STRATEGY 6—HOOK UP AND STAY HOOKED

While you shouldn't measure your fishing success entirely by how many fish you catch, if you don't hook up and stay hooked, you're not catching . . . only fishing.

- Use the right-sized hook and make sure it's sharp.
- Make sure your knots and connections are tied correctly.
- Match your rod and reel to the fish.
- Set the hook with a strip-strike.
- Once the fish is hooked, the next job is clearing the line.
- Control the line and maintain tension.
- Use light drag pressure (1 to 3 pounds).
- Use your hands to increase line pressure.
- While fighting, either the fish should be taking line or you should be retrieving line.
- Only put a fish on the reel if it earns it.
- Apply maximum side pressure to wear down the fish.
- Use surging waves to help carry the fish onto the beach.
- Safely unhook, carefully revive, then release fish.
- Remember, don't be mean . . . release them when they're green.

PLAN
YOUR FISHING

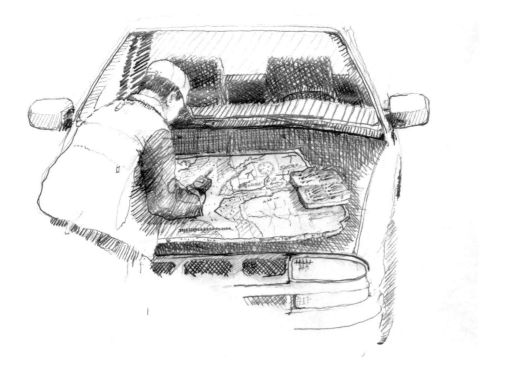

Like many things in life, as in fishing you can just wait, take your chances, and see what happens—or you can have vision, forethought, and plan your future to increase your odds of success. Fishing will always be fishing, and there will never be any guarantees—if there were it would be called "catching." As I have described in this book, many variables affect the quality of fishing in any given location at any given time. However, if you do your homework and plan your fishing, you stand a much better chance at being successful.

195

Let's take Joe Flyfisherman, for example.

Joe lives in Pennsylvania and plans to fly fish while vacationing along the New Jersey shore during mid-July. He's very excited about his vacation, especially having the opportunity and time to fly fish in salt water for striped bass now that his kids are all grown up. Without the kids, it will be just him, the fish, and his wife, in that order . . . or so he thinks. Each morning, Joe has an early breakfast, hits the suds by 8 A.M., and fishes hard for three or four hours. He returns to the summerhouse, has lunch with his wife, walks the beach, takes a little swim, and then hits the suds again with rod in hand. He fishes for two or three hours more until it starts to get dark, when he calls it quits for the day to take his wife for a nice dinner. He's a bit frustrated after witnessing a bluefish blitz just off the beach, but it was way too windy for casting a 7-weight. Another 20 feet or so and he could have caught a ton of them—that is, if he was able to keep his floating fly line from getting washed up on the beach and tangling around his feet all the time. These were some nice 5- to 8-pounders. Boy, they would have been fun to catch. The bait fishermen out on the jetties seemed to be catching quite a few fish, but after the cuts, scrapes, and bruises he suffered the day before slipping on the slimy jetty rocks, there was no way Joe was going to try fishing on those rocks again. By the end of the week, Joe had essentially gone fishless with the exception of a few small snapper blues. He had a few larger bluefish take his fly but they kept on cutting him off. Still, he did enjoy casting the long rod and the time on the water.

Let's take a look at Joe's situation and make some observations relating to his planning—or lack thereof.

- If Joe wanted to target striped bass off New Jersey, July was not the best month to do so. Spring or fall would have been much better (May; October through December); stripers are migrating through and can be found in larger numbers. With no kids, Joe and his wife may have enjoyed the peaceful quiet fall along the beautiful Jersey shore much more. There would have been far fewer people and far more fish.
- There are a fair number of resident stripers that stay in Jersey waters throughout the summer months. However, stripers are primarily nocturnal feeders during this time period. Peak times to fish for stripers are

during low light (at night, one hour before sunset, and/or one hour after sunrise). Joe would probably have had some success fishing for stripers during these times, but instead he started when the better fishing was quitting and ended his day just when the better fishing was about to start.

- A 9- or even a 10-weight rod is necessary when fishing the surf. Wind of 10 to 15 mph is the norm. A heavier 9- or 10-weight outfit could have enabled Joe to punch through the wind to reach the blitzing blues. Joe brought only a 7-weight outfit, though. It would have been okay for fishing the back bays, but not for the surf.

- Joe was also using a floating line to fish from the beach and through the waves. A floating line would have been fine for fishing from the jetty in a very light surf, especially at night when stripers feed close to jetties and in the wash of the waves. Perhaps a better choice would have been a shooting-head setup that would have enabled Joe to switch line weights. A weighted or intermediate shooting head sinks below the waves, and the running line cuts through the waves rather than getting washed in like a floating line.

- While stripers usually aren't a consistently good target during summer daylight hours along Jersey, summer flounder or fluke are reliable fish for the fly rodder. A 9- or 10-weight outfit and a sinking line could have put him onto aggressive fluke and salvaged Joe's fishing vacation.

- Joe could also have benefited by using a stripping basket to keep his line out of the surf and away from his feet. It would also have increased his casting distance.

- It appears that Joe tried walking on the slippery jetty without the aid of spiked or metal-cleat shoes. He wasn't prepared with the right safety equipment. He's lucky to have gotten away with only some minor scrapes and bruises.

- Joe did not anticipate running into bluefish with their very sharp dentures. Heavier mono tippets or stainless-steel metal leaders would have kept him connected.

Some suggestions for Joe's next striper trip:
- Do some preliminary research on the area you plan to fish. Find out about the gamefish found, where best to fish, when best to fish (day and time of year), what equipment is necessary, and what tactics to use. Check bookstores to see if there are any books that cover the area. Visit

some Web sites with message boards and post a few questions. In this
case Joe would have benefited greatly by reading Jim Freda's new book,
Fishing the New Jersey Coast.

➤ Find out what other gamefish are found in the area you plan to fish.
They can provide a great alternative. In this case, Joe could have also
possibly targeted weakfish in the back bays at night and fluke/flounder
in the surf during the day.

➤ If you aren't familiar with an area, it's a great idea to hire a guide. Most of
us only go on vacation once a year. Splurge a little. A shore guide in this
case probably would have put Joe onto fish, but would have also showed
him where and how to fish. For the rest of his vacation, Joe would have
been better educated and more likely to catch fish. An alternative would
have been to charter a boat captain. Many areas in the back bays hold
stripers, and weakfish can be taken with sinking lines in nearby
Delaware Bay, but most of these areas are only accessible with a boat.

➤ The best summer striper fishing can be found along the New England
coast. If summer is the only time Joe can vacation and he's really interested in targeting stripers, then he might want to investigate vacationing someplace like Cape Cod or Martha's Vineyard, if it fits his budget.

Hopefully, this example emphasizes the importance of planning your fishing. Planning should not be limited to just special vacation trips. Every
fishing trip, whether it's for two hours or two weeks, should start with planning. All fishing is special. Plan you magical moments.

IDENTIFY YOUR TARGET—
WHAT DO YOU WANT TO FISH FOR?

One of the most significant differences between fresh- and saltwater fishing is that freshwater fish essentially live year-round in the streams, rivers,
ponds, and lakes where you fish for them. Not so for many saltwater
species found in temperate and cold-water fisheries. Many of these species
such as striped bass, bluefish, gray sea trout, and salmon are migratory
and swim great distances following their preferred water temperatures and
baitfish. Other species such as false albacore, snook, and redfish may swim
far fewer miles, but they do oscillate back and forth between different
waters. Along North Carolina's Outer Banks, for example, false albacore
move in and out from the nearby Gulf Stream depending upon local water
conditions and the availability of baitfish. Yes, fall is the most reliable time

to fish for them in North Carolina's waters, but when the conditions are right they can show up throughout the winter and spring months as well. Rob Paisfield of Harkers Island Fishing Center fame told me about some terrific false albacore fishing he had in the Cape Lookout area during the winter and spring of 2001. In southwest Florida in the Ten Thousand Islands area of Everglades National Park, snook and redfish work their way into the backcountry during the colder months of the year in search of warmer waters and bait. When warm weather returns in spring, they work their way back out into the shallow bays and near-shore waters. Just remember one important point—no matter how good an angler you are, you can't catch fish if they're not there.

Because different species of fish may be found in different locations at different times, planning your fishing becomes a critically important strategy for ensuring your fishing success. Though you may just be fishing your local waters, give thought to what you will be fishing for, especially if you would like to target a specific species. After doing your research, you may find that the stripers you would have liked to target are not running at this time of year. Instead, you may find that weakfishing in the back bays has been excellent in the evening and early morning.

Even planning local fishing excursions is important, but planning fishing trips for species outside your realm of knowledge and comfort is downright critical. You'll really need to do your homework when planning to fish for such species. If you lived in the Florida Keys, bonefishing would be nothing unusual. Minimal planning would be required. However, if you're not from the Keys and have not gone bonefishing before, a high degree of planning and preparation would be recommended.

Sometimes, of course, planning a vacation is not entirely in your control—if you're married, for instance, or you're traveling on business and want to try to get in some fly fishing. Then the process of planning may be a little different. Since you already know where you'll be going, the next thing you'll need to do is find out what kinds of different saltwater game species are available in the area and which ones you wish to target.

DEVELOPING YOUR FISHING PLAN

The following is a helpful guide for planning your fishing. By doing some preliminary research in answering the questions below, you'll be provided with a wealth of information that will help you plan your fishing and thereby increase your odds of success.

COMMON IN-SHORE GAMEFISH MATRIX

GAME-FISH	GEOGRAPHICAL RANGE	HABITAT PREFERENCES	TYPES OF FORAGE	FLY SUGGESTION
Striped Bass	Atlantic: North Carolina to New England Pacific: California to Washington	Areas with current and structure, sand flats, surf, back bays and creeks, open near coastal waters when migrating & feeding on bait schools	Small to very large baitfish, crabs, squid, shrimp, marine worms	Deceiver, Clouser, Half & Half, Pretender, Jiggy Fly, Slab Fly, Snake Fly, CreaseFly, Gurgler, Poppers
Bluefish	New England to Florida	Areas with current and structure, sand flats, surf, open near coastal waters when migrating & feeding on bait schools	Small to very large baitfish, squid	Deceiver, Clouser, Half & Half, Pretender, Jiggy Fly, Crease Fly, Popper
False Albacore	New England to Caribbean	Areas of strong currents with deep water nearby, inlets, surf, open near coastal waters when feeding on bait schools, behind trawlers	Mostly small baitfish like silversides but will take larger baitfish like finger mullet	Silverside Surf Candies, Alba Clouser, Half & Half, Mike's Silverside-In, Pretender, Rain Bait, Crease Fly
Bonito	Southern New England to Mid-Atlantic States British Columbia to Mexico	Areas of strong currents with adjacent deep water, inlets, surf, open near coastal waters when feeding on bait schools	Small baitfish like silversides & anchovies	Silverside Surf Candies, Alba Clouser, Half & Half, Mike's Silverside-In, Pretender, Rain Bait, Crease Fly
Gray Trout/ Weakfish	New England to Carolinas	Surf, inlets, large bays, areas of structure and current, back bays and creeks	Small to medium sized baitfish, crabs, shrimp and marine worms	Deciever, Clouser, Jiggy Fly, Pretender, Ultra Shrimp, Crease Fly, Gurgler
Speckled Trout	Mid-Atlantic States along coast to Texas	Protected bays, inlets and estuaries with sandy bottoms, grass beds and clear water	Small to medium sized baitfish, crabs, shrimp	Deciever, Clouser, Jiggy Fly, Pretender

COMMON IN-SHORE GAMEFISH MATRIX

GAME-FISH	GEOGRAPHICAL RANGE	HABITAT PREFERENCES	TYPES OF FORAGE	FLY SUGGESTION
Spanish Mac	Chesapeake Bay South to Florida and Gulf of Mexico	Open near coastal waters, surf, large bays	Small to medium sized baitfish	Deceiver, Clouser, Alba Clouser, Pretender, Surf Candy, Popper
Redfish	Virginia to Florida, along Gulf Coast from Florida to Texas	Along beaches and in the surf, inlets, channel edges, back bays, oyster bars	Small to medium sized baitfish, shrimp	Seaducer, Deceiver, Clouser, Dalberg Diver, Spoon Fly, Bamboozle, Bend Back
Jack Crevalle	North Carolina to Florida, Gulf of Mexico	In the surf and along beaches, inlets, bays, structure, behind trawlers	Medium to large baitfish	Deceiver, Clouser, Half & Half, Pretenders, Jiggy Fly, Crease Fly, Popper
Snook	American tropics and sub-tropics	Areas of structure and current, along beaches in Summer, inlets, rivers, back bays, mangrove edges	Small to medium sized baitfish, shrimp	Seaducer, Deceiver, Clouser, Dalberg Diver, Bamboozle, Bend Back
Tarpon	Mid-Atlantic States to Florida, Bahamas, Caribbean	Medium depth flats, along beaches, inlets, rivers, back bays, canals, mangrove edges	Shrimp, crabs	Key's Tarpon Fly, Cockroach, Dalberg Diver, Deceiver
Bonefish	Shallow tropical and subtropical waters worldwide	Shallow flats of either hard or soft bottoms	Shrimp, crabs, small baitfish	Gotcha, Clouser, Bamboozle, Silly Legs, Ultra Shrimp
Permit	Florida, Gulf of Mexico, Bahamas, Caribbean	Medium depth flats of hard or soft bottoms	Crabs, crabs, crabs	Merkin, Puff, McCrab, Samson's Fighting Crab

Where are the fish typically found geographically? Answering this question will give you a quick indication of where the fish you wish to target are generally found, or it can tell you what fish are generally found in the location where you wish to fish. This is only a general indicator. You'll need to do more research to find out specific locations that offer the best opportunity. Remember, you can't catch them if they aren't there.

Are there certain geographic regions that offer better opportunities than others? The answer to this question will help you fine-tune the answer to the question above and is of particular importance if you want to maximize your chances. With many species, certain geographic regions offer prime habitat and abundant food. These regions will therefore attract larger-than-normal numbers of fish. The more fish are available, the more opportunities you'll have. New Providence Island (Nassau) in the Bahamas is located in the Tropics but does not have expansive shallow flats to support a large population of bonefish. Andros Island, on the other hand—a short distance away—has extensive shallow flats and supports an enormous population of bonefish. The downside is that Andros is more rural in nature and does not have much in the way of nightlife. Grand Bahamas Island

Areas along our coasts see annual migrations of fish like this nice Delaware Bay striper.

(Freeport) might be a better alternative if you're considering a beach-and-fish vacation with your spouse. The good news is that Grand Bahamas Island also has extensive flats, a healthy population of bones and guides for hire.

What times of the year are they found in these locations? Are they migratory or are they found in these areas year-round? As mentioned previously, many saltwater species are migratory and/or may oscillate between different areas. One of the most reliable areas to catch big striped bass is along the Chesapeake Bay Bridge Tunnel and along the North Carolina coast during December and January when they typically winter over. However, during much of the year from April through September stripers are only present in moderate numbers and sizes.

What times of the year offer the best opportunity for which areas? Knowing the times of the year when fish are present in the largest numbers will give you the best window of opportunity to plan your trip. Of course there are no guarantees when it comes to fishing, but planning to be in a specific area at the peak time will certainly put the odds in your favor.

What time of the day is it best to fish for them? Despite popular belief, not all fish feed when it is convenient for us. Thankfully, many do, and we can fish for them during daylight hours. Certain species like striped bass, sea trout, and snook have a preference for feeding in low-light situations, especially during warmer conditions. If you're not fishing at night or miss the early-morning bite, you might be out of luck. However, fishing for these species at night around lighted bridges and docks can provide some of the most reliable action during these times. When targeting such species as bones, permit, tarpon, and even stripers on the flats, light becomes essential for sight fishing.

What do they feed on? Knowing the types of bait that the species you are targeting potentially feed on will of course give you an indication of what types, colors, and sizes of flies you will need to be prepared with.

What will be the prevalent bait when you plan to fish? Knowing the specific baits that will be most prevalent when you plan to fish will give you an edge in having the right flies. Having an assortment of these flies in varying colors and sizes will greatly increase your odds of success if you find fish.

How do they feed? How a particular fish feeds is of particular importance since it will indicate not only where you may find them but also how to present a fly to entice them to strike. Snook and stripers, for example, like to ambush prey. Stripers are also found in large schools that surround pods of bait and force them to the surface, where they will feed aggressively. Bonefish and redfish, on the other hand, have inferior or downturned mouths and are primarily bottom feeders.

What habitat do they prefer? Knowing the preferred habitat of a species will give you a major advantage in locating fish. Snook like to hide out under the overhanging branches of mangroves. From its shady retreat, the snook will be able to easily see any baitfish or fly that happens by. Like stripers, snook also prefer to lie in wait in and around structure like pilings, jetties or bridge supports, especially where there is a relatively strong current. Additionally, both species can often be found working the outer beaches in search of baitfish (spring and summer for snook). This could provide a good alternative for wading if you don't have access to a boat.

Local weather conditions can create wonderful fishing opportunities. Just off the Highlands of Sandy Hook, New Jersey, the water churns with huge numbers of migrating fall stripers feeding on rainbait near the surface. A light but steady northeast wind and overcast skies helped set the stage for a phenomenal day of fishing.

What weight rod and reel is recommended? Selecting the right weight of rod and reel is important in being able to cast effectively in windy conditions and/or using larger flies, to present the fly softly in delicate situations and to be able to fight the fish you seek fairly.

What types of lines are recommended? Selecting the right fly line is essential in maximizing your presentation, as discussed in strategy 5. It's also a good idea to have your reel and spare spool or reel loaded with different lines—perhaps a floater for surface action and an intermediate for getting down a little. If you're planning to fish areas of deeper water, it's a good idea to be prepared with not only an intermediate line but also several sinking lines of varying sink rates to get your fly down to where the fish are holding.

What fly patterns and sizes are most effective? Knowing what bait the fish feed on will be a good indicator of what flies will likely be effective. Still, it's always helpful to take the advice of other experienced anglers regarding what flies are likely to be successful.

FINE-TUNING YOUR FISHING PLAN

Here are some additional things to do to fine-tune your plan and increase your odds of success:

Check with friends, Web sites, and other sources for the latest fishing reports. Saltwater fish are always on the move. An area that was producing fish several days ago may not have fish today. Try to get the latest information from the most reliable source. Fishing buddies are always best. If you don't have a friend who fishes the area, then try a number of different fly shops and/or fishing Web sites that may have recent posts concerning the fishing in the area. Remember to search both fly-fishing and non-fly-fishing sites. You'll be surprised how often bait and surf fishermen will pass along comments about fish in the surf, busting fish, or bait in the area that could provide a good a lead on where best to fish. If you find similar information on different Web sites from different anglers, you'll have a good indication that the information is reliable.

Check local and marine weather forecasts. As mentioned previously, weather is critically important to fishing and personal safety, especially if you're planning to fish from a boat, jetty, or surf. Weather conditions can

Low-light conditions and warm early-spring days are magic times for stripers. Plan
your fishing trip accordingly.

change unexpectedly. Check your favorite Web site for weather and marine conditions at least a week beforehand if your fishing involves significant land or air travel. This is especially important when planning to fish tropical or subtropical areas. Tropical storms or cold fronts can put a serious damper on the fishing. It may be better to reschedule your trip. Check the weather and marine conditions again the day and morning before you depart to be on the safe side. You may need to reschedule or alter your original plans. Windy, choppy, and downright snotty conditions can have some of the best fishing. However, fishing in these conditions is not everyone's cup of tea, and safety must always come first. As we all know, weather forecasts can often be inaccurate, so sometimes you just have to go and see what happens. Sometimes it's a bust, but other times you may just have one of your best fishing days ever.

Confirm tidal information for the areas and moon phase you plan to fish. Tidal conditions are critical to most saltwater fishing. Check and confirm the times for high and low tides. This is of particular importance if the areas you plan to visit fish better on one tide change than the other. Certain highly productive flats for bonefish, permit, tarpon, and stripers are dry at low tide and can only be fished with the rising tide. Spring tides in fall trigger a mass migration of baitfish from the back bays to near-shore waters. When this happens, fishing improves dramatically. Unless you have a lot of time to waste, don't just show up and hope for the best . . . have some foresight . . . plan for the best.

Confirm water temperature and clarity (if applicable). Confirming the water temperature and/or water clarity is often important during transition times of the year for many coastal areas. Increases and decreases in water temperature when transitioning from winter to spring and summer to fall trigger spawning and migratory urges for many inshore species of fish. A few warm days in spring may be all that's necessary to bring tarpon or stripers into the shallows. With times of weather transition come winds and rains that can dramatically increase the turbidity of inshore waters, making fishing difficult and catching a near impossibility.

Identify primary and alternate fishing areas to target. Review navigational charts of the area you're planning to fish and identify a number of primary locations to target. Whether you're fishing from a boat or shore, navigational charts will provide you with a wealth of information concerning the nature of the water—indicating channels, drop-offs, rips, bars, sloughs, sod banks, and more that will likely hold fish. Since there are no guarantees when it comes to fishing or the weather, it's a good idea to plan for alternate fishing locations just in case the primary ones don't pan out.

Check and pack your rods and reels. If you're planning a major trip, it's always a good idea to lay out the rods and reels you plan to take and give them a good close inspection. Check the reel seats, guides, tip-top, and wraps for any potential defects. I like to spray the guides and reel seat with WD-40 for added protection against the corrosive effects of salt water. Inspect the drag of your reels to make sure it operates smoothly; lubricate as necessary. Make sure all screws are tight. When complete, spray the all metal surfaces with WD-40 for added protection. When fishing from a boat, I typically bring four to six rods of varying weights depending upon the types and sizes of fish I am likely to encounter. Matching the rod to the size and fight of the fish maximizes the experience. For many near-shore boat-fishing situations along the northern and mid-Atlantic coasts, it's also a good idea to have multiple rods set up with different flies and lines (floater, intermediate, 250-grain, 550-grain) so you are ready for just about any situation at a moment's notice. If you are fishing from shore, you should have multiple shooting heads of varying sink rates that you can also change quickly.

Check your backing. Depending upon the frequency of use and how well you clean your lines, you should change your backing every two to three years. Check your backing for condition and any signs of wear and replace if you have any doubts as to its reliability.

Check and pack your fly lines, shooting heads, and running lines. Load your reels and any spare spools with the fly lines/shooting heads that will match the fishing conditions you are most likely to encounter. For flats and shallow water up to 3 feet deep, a floating and intermediate line will cover most situations. When fishing deeper near-shore waters with areas of strong currents and wave action, sinking lines/shooting heads of varying weights will be necessary to keep your fly down.

Check and pack your leader and tippet material. I like to tie up my leaders before time so they are all taken care of and loaded on the reels I plan to use. This minimizes any setup time and potential mistakes on the water,

Fishing the surf along Delaware's coast. Stripers and bluefish will often feed right in the suds just a short cast away.

GAMEFISH TACKLE & EQUIPMENT MATRIX

GAME-FISH	ROD WT.	REEL BACKING CAPACITY	FLY LINE(S)	LEADER LENGTH	CLASS TIPPET	SHOCK TIPPET
Striped Bass	7-8 9-10	20# 100-150 yds 30# 175-250 yds	Floating Intermediate Sinking (200-800)	7-12 ft 3-4' sinking	12-20 lb.	N/A
Bluefish	7-8 9-10	20# 100-150 yds 30# 175-250 yds	Floating Intermediate Sinking (200-550)	7-9 ft 3-4' sinking	12-20 lb.	Wire
False Albacore	8-9 10-12	20# 150-200 yds 30# 200-300 yds	Floating Intermediate Sinking (200-550)	7-10 ft 3-4' sinking	12-20 lb.	N/A
Bonito	8-9 9-10	20# 150-200 yds 30# 200-250 yds	Floating Intermediate Sinking (200-350)	7-10ft 3-4' sinking	12-20 lb.	N/A
Gray Trout/ Weakfish	7-8 9	20# 100-150 yds 30# 150-200 yds	Floating Intermediate Sinking (200-550)	7-9 ft 3-4' sinking	10-20 lb.	N/A
Speckled Trout	7-8	20# 100-150 yds	Floating Intermediate Sinking (200-350)	7-12 ft 4-6' sinking	10-20 lb.	N/A
Spanish Mac	7-8 9	20# 100-150 yds 30# 150-200 yds	Floating Intermediate Sinking (200-350)	7-9 ft 4-6' sinking	10-15 lb.	15-20 # Mono or Wire

GAMEFISH TACKLE & EQUIPMENT MATRIX

GAME-FISH	ROD WT.	REEL BACKING CAPACITY		FLY LINE(S)	LEADER LENGTH	CLASS TIPPET	SHOCK TIPPET
Redfish	7-8 9	20# 30#	100-150 yds 150-200 yds	Floating Intermediate Sinking (200-350)	7-9 ft 4-6' sinking	10-20 lb.	N/A
Jack Crevalle	8-9 10-12	20# 30#	150-200 yds 200-300 yds	Floating Intermediate Sinking (200-550)	7-9 ft 4-6' sinking	12-20 lb.	40-70 # Mono
Snook	7-8 9-10	20# 30#	100-150 yds 150-200 yds	Floating Intermediate Sinking (200-350)	7-9 ft 4-6' sinking	12-20 lb.	40-70 # Mono
Tarpon	7-8 9-10 12-13	20# 30# 30#	100-150 yds 175-250 yds 250-350 yds	Floating Intermediate Sinking (200-350)	9-12 ft 5-6' sinking	12-20 lb.	40-100 # Mono
Bonefish	7-8 9	30# 30#	150-200 yds 200-250 yds	Floating Intermediate	10-15 ft	10-15 lb.	N/A
Permit	8-9 10	30# 30#	150-200 yds 200-300 yds	Floating Intermediate	9-12 ft	12-15 lb.	N/A

NOTE: Tackle and equipment should correspond to the size of the fish you are pursuing. Lighter weight rods, backing and class tippets and less backing capacity are for smaller fish while heavier weight rods, backing and class tippets and more backing capacity are for larger more powerful fish.

when things can get a little hectic. Having the necessary leader and tippet material enables you to tie up any new leaders and change to different tippets when fish get finicky. Not having fluorocarbon tippet material or stainless-steel wire on the water or far down the beach from your vehicle in a time of need could put a serious damper on your fishing.

Check, buy or tie, and pack your flies. It's important to do your research beforehand if needed to ensure you know what flies and sizes will most likely be effective.

Check and pack your gear and safety devices. Make a list of the additional gear you will need, such as waders, stripping basket, bibs, boats, corkers, flashlight, compass, personal flotation device, and so on, and make sure you pack everything up and take it along. You may have your rod, but without an essential piece of gear, you may not be able to fish.

Check and pack your radio and/or cell phone. Whether fixed on a boat or a handheld unit, a VHF radio provides up-to-date marine weather forecasts and access to the U.S. Coast Guard in case of emergencies. By monitoring certain channels on VHF radios, you can possibly learn updated fishing in-

Research and select the right flies for your trip. Choose the vital few.

formation listening to other fishermen. Sometimes they give locations away and sometimes they don't, but you won't know unless you listen. Both VHF radios and cell phones can be used as effective communication devices in emergencies and for holding a confidential conversation with your fishing buddies concerning the latest fishing. For waters that I fish frequently with friends, we usually "code" the chart with numbered locations that only we know. This way we can talk openly on the radio without worrying about giving the location away to numerous other fishermen.

Check the operation of your vehicle or boat and safety devices. Remember Murphy's Law, which states anything that can go wrong will go wrong at the most inopportune time. Needless to say, without your vehicle and/or boat, you probably won't be able to fish. If your fishing time is important to you, protect it by checking over your vehicle and/or boat to make sure everything is operating properly and you have all your necessary safety devices (cell phone, radio, flash light, PFD, flares). Remember . . . safety first!

Here are some resources where you can get the information you need to properly plan your fishing:

Prepare and rig up several rods with different weighted lines and flies before you go fishing. Time spent rigging on the water is lost fishing time.

- Network of fishing buddies.
- Local fly or tackle shops.
- Web sites and message boards covering your waters.
- Local guide service (if you're thinking about booking a trip).
- Fly-fishing books.
- Local newspapers and fishing magazines.
- Previous editions of saltwater fly-fishing magazines.

Of course, as you become more experienced in fishing certain locations and/or species, the planning process becomes easier and almost transparent. You'll find that you will develop good planning habits that will increase your odds of success.

Just remember the 5 P's: Prior Planning Prevents Poor Performance.

Follow these seven strategies to increase your saltwater fly-fishing success and enjoy the magic moments.

STRATEGY 7—PLAN YOUR FISHING

Like many things in life, in fishing you can just wait, take your chances, and see what happens—or you can have vision, forethought, and plan your future to increase your odds of success. Fishing will always be fishing, and there will never be any guarantees. As I have described in this book, many variables affect the quality of fishing in any given location at any given time. However, if you do your homework and plan your fishing, you stand a much better chance at being successful.

Develop your plan by answering the following:

- What fish do you want to target?
- Where are they typically found geographically?
- Are there certain geographic regions that offer better opportunities than others?
- What times of the year are they found in these locations? Are they migratory or are they found in these areas year-round?
- What times of year offer the best opportunity for which areas?
- What times of day is it best to fish for them?
- What do they feed on?
- What will be the prevalent bait when you plan to fish?
- How do they feed?
- What habitat do they prefer?
- What weight rod and reel is recommended?
- What types of lines are recommended?
- What fly patterns and profiles are most effective?

Fine-tune your fishing plan by doing the following:

- Check with friends, Web sites, and other sources for the latest fishing reports.
- Check local and marine weather forecasts.
- Confirm tidal information for the areas and moon phase you plan to fish.
- Confirm water temperature and clarity (if applicable).

- Identify primary and alternate fishing areas to target.
- Check and pack your rods and reels.
- Check your backing and replace if necessary.
- Check and pack your fly lines, shooting heads, and running lines.
- Check and pack your leader and tippet materials.
- Check, buy or tie, and pack your flies.
- Check and pack your gear and safety devices.
- Check and pack your radio and/or cell phone.
- Check the operation of your vehicle or boat and safety devices.

SEVEN STRATEGIES FOR SUCCESS

1. Learn Continuously

2. Become a Proficient Caster

3. Spend Time on the Water

4. Use the Right Fly

5. Maximize Your Presentation

6. Hook Up and Stay Hooked

7. Plan Your Fishing

FLY FISHING RESOURCES

REF	BOOK SAMPLING	AUTHOR	PUBLISHER
1	Advanced Fly Casting, 1995 (Lefty's Little Library)	Kreh	Odysseus Editions
2	Advanced Fly Fishing Techniques, 1992	Kreh	Delacorte Press
3	Backcountrry Fly Fishing in Slat Water, 1995	Swisher & Richards	Lyons & Burford
4	Bonefishing with a Fly, 1992	Kaufmann	Western Fisherman's Press
5	Fly Fishing for Bonefish, 1993	Brown	Lyons & Burford
6	Fly Fishing in Salt Water, 1986	Kreh	Lyons & Burford
7	Flyrodding Florida Salt, 1995	Kuminski	Argonaut
8	Fly Fishing Offshore, 1998	Preble	The Fisherman
9	Fly-Fishing The Flats, 1999	Beck	Stackpole Books
10	Fly Rodding The Coast, 1995	Mitchell	Stackpole Books
11	Fly Fishing The Tide Water, 1995	Earnhardt	Lyons & Burford
12	Inshore Fly Fishing, 1992	Tabory	Lyons & Burford
13	Innovative Saltwater Flies, 1999	Veverka	Stackpole Books
14	L.L. Bean Fly Fishing For Striped Bass Handbook, 1998	Burns	The Lyons Press
15	Lou Tabory's Guide to Saltwater Baits & Their Imitations, 1995	Tabory	Lyons & Burford
16	Modern Fly Casting, 1995 (Lefty's Little Library)	Kreh	Odysseus Editions
17	Modern Fly-Tying Materials, 1995	Talleur	Lyons & Burford
18	Permit On a Fly, 1996	Samson	Stackpole Books
19	Pop Fleyes, 2001	Jaworowski-Popovics	Stackpole Books
20	Presentation, 1995	Borger	Tomorrow River Press
21	Presenting The Fly, 1999	Kreh	The Lyons Press
22	Prey, 1995	Richards	Lyons & Burford
23	Reeds's Nautical Almanac (specify East Coast or West Coast)		Thomas Reed Publications
24	Saltwater Angler's Guide to The Southeast, 1999	Newman	Wilderness Adventures Press
25	Saltwater Fly Patterns, 1995	Kreh	Lyons & Burford
26	Solving Fly-Casting Problems, 2000	Kreh	The Lyons Press
27	Striper Moon, 1994	Abrames	Frank Amato Publications

28	Stripers and Streamers, 1996	Bondorew	Frank Amato Publications
29	Stripers on the Fly, 1999	Tabory	The Lyons Press
30	The Cast, 1992	Jaworowski	Stackpole Books
31	Troubleshooting The Cast, 1999	Jaworowski	Stackpole Books

REF	MAGAZINE SAMPLING	FREQUENCY	PUBLISHER
32	Fly Fishing in Salt Waters	Bi-monthly	World Publications
33	Saltwater Fly Fishing	Bi-monthly	Abenaki
34	Fly Fisherman	Monthly	PRIMEDIA
35	Fly Rod & Reel	Bi-monthly	Down East Enterprise

REF	VIDEO SAMPLING	AUTHOR	PRODUCER
36	Dynamics of Fly Casting	Wulff	Miracle Productions
37	Fly Casting with Lefty Kreh	Kreh	Tomorrow River Press
38	Practical Fly Casting	Beck Production	A Reel Resources
39	The Essence of Flycasting	Krieger	Club Pacific
40	The Essence of Flycasting II	Krieger	Club Pacific

REF	WEB SITE SAMPLING	ADDRESSES
41	Atlantic Saltwater Flyrodders	www.aswf.org
42	Basic Guide to Saltwater Fly Fishing in Southwest Florida	www.marco-island-florida.com/don/home.htm
43	Federation of Fly Fishers	www.fedflyfishers.org
44	Flat Out Saltwater Fly Fishing (North Carolina)	www.outerbanksflyfishing.com
45	Fly-A-Way Guide Service (Mid-Atlantic/Northeast)	www.fly-a-way.com
46	Fly Fishing in Salt Waters Magazine	www.flyfishinsalt.com
47	Fly Fishing Southwest Texas	www.sightcast1.com/fly
48	Offshoreweather.com	www.offshoreweather.com
49	Orvis	www.orvis.com
50	Redington	www.redington.com
51	Reel-Time (Northeast)	www.reel-time.com
52	Shore Catch Guide Service (New Jersey)	www.shorecatch.com
53	Stripers On Line	www.stripersonline.com
54	The Florida Keys Fly Fishing School	www.floridakeysoutfitters.com
55	WWW Tide and Current Predictor	http://tbone.biol.sc.edu/tide/sitesel.html
56	Weather Underground	www.wunderground.com
57	Tidalfish.com	www.tidalfish.com

USING THE REFERENCE MATRIX: To determine which categories of information are covered by the resources listed above, simply refer to the COLUMN under the matching reference number listed on the top of the matrix. To determine which resources cover a specific category, simply pick a category along the left margin and follow the ROW across. Note: This reference matrix is only intended to be a guide.

KEY: B=Book M=Magazine V=Video W=Web Site

REFERENCE MATRIX

REF	1	2	3	4	5	6	7	8	9	10	11	12	13	14	15	16	17	18	19	20	21	22	23	24	25	26	27	28	29	30	31	32	33	34	35	36	37	38	39	40	41	42	43	44	45	46	47	48	49	50	51	52	53	54	55	56	57
Rods/Reels		B	B	B	B	B	B	B	B	B	B	B	B	B							B			B			B	B	B	B	B	M	M	M	M							W	W			W				W	W							W
Lines/Leaders		B	B	B	B	B	B	B	B	B	B	B	B	B							B			B			B	B	B	B		M	M	M	M							W	W			W				W	W							
Knots		B		B	B	B	B	B	B	B	B	B									B									B		M	M	M	M						W					W				W	W							
Gear		B	B	B	B	B	B	B	B	B	B	B	B	B							B								B	B		M	M	M	M										W	W			W	W					W			
Techniques		B	B	B	B	B	B	B	B	B	B	B	B	B			B				B			B			B	B	B	B		M	M	M	M								W	W	W		W	W		W		W	W	W					W
Casting	B	B	B	B	B	B	B	B	B	B	B	B				B				B	B				B							M	M	M	M	V	V	V	V			W	W	W	W	W	W						W	W				
Presentation		B	B	B	B	B	B	B	B	B	B	B					B	B	B		B			B			B	B	B	B		M	M	M	M	V	V	V	V			W					W				W		W	W		W	W	W			W
Flies		B	B	B	B	B	B	B	B	B	B	B	B	B	B		B	B	B		B	B		B	B		B	B	B	B		M	M	M	M							W	W				W				W		W	W		W	W				W
Hooking/Fighting		B		B				B	B	B		B					B	B										B		B		M	M	M	M																								
Weather				B	B	B				B				B													B	B	B	B													W			W		W	W					W		W		W
Water Conditions				B	B	B	B				B			B													B	B	B	B													W			W		W	W		W			W		W	W	
Tides		B	B	B	B	B	B			B	B	B		B							B		B	B			B	B	B	B										W		W				W		W	W		W	W	W	W		W		
Fishing Reports																																								W	W		W	W			W				W	W	W	W				W
Message Board																																													W								W				W
Northeast						B		B	B	B		B	B														B	B	B	B		M	M	M	M										W	W	W				W	W						W
Mid-Atlantic						B	B	B	B	B	B	B	B	B													B	B	B			M	M	M	M					W			W	W	W	W				W	W	W		W				W
Southeast						B	B	B	B	B	B													B						B		M	M	M	M								W	W		W				W								W
Gulf States			B	B	B	B	B		B	B																	B					M	M	M	M												W	W			W					W			W
Tropics			B	B	B	B			B	B							B															M	M	M	M																W								W
West Coast						B																								B		M	M	M	M								W		W	W				W								W
Flats		B		B	B	B			B			B	B	B			B										B	B	B	B		M	M	M	M								W			W				W	W				W			W
Shorelines				B	B	B	B	B	B	B	B	B															B	B	B			M	M	M	M								W			W				W	W	W						W
Estuaries			B		B	B	B		B	B	B	B									B						B	B	B			M	M	M	M								W			W				W	W	W			W			W
Open Water		B		B		B		B	B	B	B	B	B	B															B			M	M	M	M								W			W				W	W	W						W
Boats		B	B	B	B	B	B	B	B	B	B	B	B	B			B				B																				W					W				W		W	W					W
Albacore/Bonito						B		B	B	B	B	B	B	B							B			B								M	M	M	M									W	W	W	W				W	W	W	W				W
Bluefish						B		B	B	B	B	B												B								M	M	M	M									W	W						W	W	W					W
Bonefish		B	B	B		B	B	B	B												B											M	M	M	M																W				W	W			W
Permit		B	B			B	B	B	B	B	B						B				B											M	M	M	M									W		W	W				W		W		W			W
Redfish					B	B	B	B	B		B	B									B			B								M	M	M	M							W		W	W	W				W		W	W		W			W
Sea Trout					B	B	B		B		B													B								M	M	M	M							W		W	W	W				W		W		W	W	W		W
Snook		B		B		B	B	B	B	B	B																					M	M	M	M							W			W	W				W								W
Stripers			B			B			B	B	B	B	B	B							B			B			B	B				M	M	M	M								W	W	W	W				W		W	W	W	W		W		W
Tarpon		B					B	B	B	B	B						B				B											M	M	M	M						W						W				W		W			W			W

INDEX